A HOUSE DIVIDED

AMERICA'S CIVIL WAR

D0067815

Perfection Learning

EDITORIAL DIRECTOR	Julie A. Schumacher
SENIOR EDITOR	Terry Ofner
EDITOR	Sherrie Voss Matthews
PERMISSIONS	Laura Pieper
REVIEWERS	Laurie Bauer
	Ann Tharnish

DESIGN AND PHOTO RESEARCH   William Seabright and Associates, Wilmette, Illinois

COVER ART LAST CIVIL WAR VETERAN 1961 Larry Rivers

ACKNOWLEDGMENTS

"At Chancellorsville," from *After The Lost War: A Narrative*. Copyright © 1988 by Andrew Hudgins. Reprinted by permission of Houghton Mifflin Company. All rights reserved.

"At Gettysburg," from *Heroes in Disguise* by Linda Pastan. Copyright © 1991 by Linda Pastan. Reprinted by permission of W. W. Norton & Company, Inc.

"Change of Heart," text by Patrick Rogers, from *People Weekly* magazine, 5/25/98. Copyright © 1998 Time, Inc. Reprinted with permission.

From *The Civil War and Reconstruction: An Eyewitness History* by Joe H. Kirchberger. Copyright © 1991 by Joe H. Kirchberger. Reprinted by permission of Facts On File, Inc.

"The Drummer Boy of Shiloh" by Ray Bradbury. First published in *The Saturday Evening Post*, April 30, 1960. Copyright © 1960 by the Curtis Publishing Co., renewed 1988 by Ray Bradbury. Reprinted by permission of Don Congdon Associates, Inc.   CONTINUED ON PAGE 151

Reinforced Library Binding ISBN-13: 978-0-7807-9320-0
Reinforced Library Binding ISBN-10: 0-7807-9320-x
Paperback ISBN-13: 978-0-7891-5152-0
Paperback ISBN-10: 0-7891-5152-9
   11 12 13 14 15   PP 12 11 10 09 08
perfectionlearning.com
Printed in the U.S.A.

WHY IS THE CIVIL WAR
A DEFINING MOMENT IN AMERICAN HISTORY?

The question above is the *essential question* that you will consider as you read this book. The literature, activities, and organization of the book will lead you to think critically about this question and to develop a deeper understanding of the American Civil War.

To help you shape your answer to the broad essential question, you will read and respond to four sections, or clusters. Each cluster addresses a specific question and thinking skill.

CLUSTER ONE 1861-1862: What were they fighting for? **ANALYZE**

CLUSTER TWO 1863: A turning point? **COMPARE/CONTRAST**

CLUSTER THREE 1864-1865: What were the costs of the war? **SUMMARIZE**

CLUSTER FOUR Thinking on your own **SYNTHESIZE**

Notice that the final cluster asks you to think independently about your answer to the essential question — *Why is the Civil War a defining moment in American history?*

A HOUSE DIVIDED
AMERICA'S CIVIL WAR

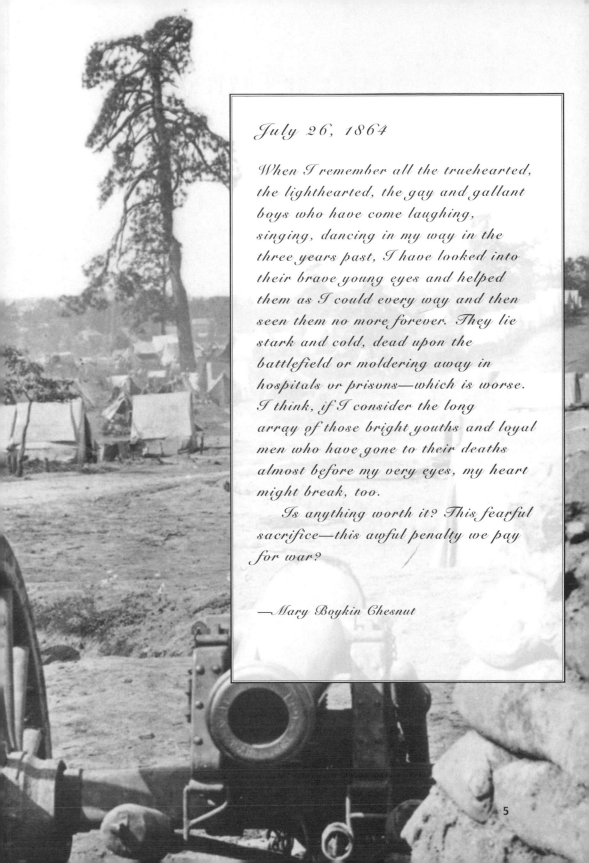

July 26, 1864

When I remember all the truehearted, the lighthearted, the gay and gallant boys who have come laughing, singing, dancing in my way in the three years past, I have looked into their brave young eyes and helped them as I could every way and then seen them no more forever. They lie stark and cold, dead upon the battlefield or moldering away in hospitals or prisons—which is worse. I think, if I consider the long array of those bright youths and loyal men who have gone to their deaths almost before my very eyes, my heart might break, too.

Is anything worth it? This fearful sacrifice—this awful penalty we pay for war?

—Mary Boykin Chesnut

TABLE OF CONTENTS

CLUSTER FOUR THINKING ON YOUR OWN 113
Thinking Skill SYNTHESIZING

THE CIVIL WAR

JOE H. KIRCHBERGER

In November 1860, Abraham Lincoln was elected president. Within two months of his election, six Southern states seceded from the Union; within six months, fighting had begun.

Lincoln's election triggered the Civil War. But tensions between the North and the South had been building for decades. The following essay outlines the issues that led to war.

James Monroe was the last president belonging to the Revolutionary generation. With its passing, the differences and dissensions within the nation became more and more apparent. Major controversies developed around the following questions and, in most of the controversies, the Northern states were on one side, the Southern states on the other:

1. **FEDERAL VERSUS STATE AUTHORITY** Could the president or a majority in Congress force a state to accept laws that went against its interest, thereby threatening the traditional independence of the individual states? The doctrine that the states were independent of one another and of the federal government, which had been pronounced by Kentucky and Virginia as early as 1798, was, since the 1820s, strongly supported by all Southern states, as a protection against too much power in the hands of the central government

Abraham Lincoln

Andrew Jackson

Henry Clay

2. PROTECTIVE TARIFF The South, mostly agrarian[1], depended on inexpensive machinery imported from Europe, while in the North the young agrarian industry wished to be protected from European, in particular British, competition. The tariffs,[2] introduced in 1824, were fiercely opposed by the Southern states, which were, however, outvoted in Congress. When the tariffs were further extended and increased in 1828 (the so-called tariff of abomination), the state of South Carolina declared that the tariffs had become too oppressive to be borne, and a state convention in November of 1832 passed an ordinance pronouncing the tariffs null and void for its territory and threatening to withdraw from the Union should the Union try to enforce the tariffs. This threat of "nullification" was immediately met by President Andrew Jackson, who announced that in case of resistance, the whole force of the Union would be used against South Carolina. An open break was finally avoided when Henry Clay, leader of the protectionists, introduced a compromise with a modified tariff that was accepted by the South.

3. THE PROBLEM OF A UNITED STATES BANK VERSUS STATE BANKS Most Southerners preferred their local banks, and here they had the support of Andrew Jackson. As the champion of the common people against privileged interests,[3] Jackson felt the United States Bank, chartered in 1816, had become too powerful and had interfered with local banks. He managed to break it up in 1836. As a result, state banks began to flourish everywhere, particularly in the Mississippi Valley, and a fluctuating paper currency ensued that favored Southwestern and Northwestern farmers, who were often in debt for their land and equipment, and worked against the Eastern seaboard establishment.

4. THE QUESTION OF WHETHER CONGRESS SHOULD ENGAGE IN BUILDING NATIONAL ROADS TO HELP SETTLEMENTS IN THE WEST Federal action for internal improvement diminished in Jacksonian times but became vigorous again when railroads

1 **agrarian:** agricultural
2 **tariffs:** taxes on imported or exported goods
3 **privileged interests:** wealthy Northern industrialists

proved to be a success and the first plans for a transcontinental railway were discussed with two routes under consideration where, again, North stood against South.

5. THE PROBLEM OF FREE LAND IN THE WEST VERSUS ITS SALE FOR REVENUE PURPOSES The policy of Congress had been to sell the land of the Western territories to settlers in small lots—or in large lots to speculators—first for $2.00, then for $1.25 per acre. This provided a substantial revenue for the federal treasury. Modest as this price seems to us now, many poor farmers or city workers who wanted to settle in the West found raising such sums difficult. Voices asking for a sharp reduction of the price and finally in favor of giving land away free in lots of 160 acres grew louder. Planters of the South opposed this movement, fearing that it would establish a supremacy of the slave-free states, particularly as more land was available in the Northwest than in the Southwest.

6. THE INSTITUTION OF SLAVERY Slavery had existed in the American colonies since the first blacks were brought to Virginia in 1619. By 1770, about one-sixth of the entire population of the colonies consisted of blacks. But in the North, climate, soil and the kind of agriculture made large-scale slavery rather unprofitable. At the end of the colonial era at least 90% of the people lived on the land, with the North producing wheat and corn; the South, tobacco, rice, sugar, indigo and, a little later, vast quantities of cotton. The South depended more and more on slave labor.

Plantation slave, 1850

The Northwest Ordinance of 1787 forbade slavery in the Northwest territory recently ceded by Britain—north of the Ohio River and east of the Mississippi. The U. S. Constitution prohibited slave trade after January 1, 1808, and slavery began to die out in the North and to dwindle slowly in the South.

Yet, with the introduction of the cotton gin, invented by Eli Whitney in 1793, the South geared into large-scale cotton production and required an ever-increasing number of slaves, particularly since

Whitney's cotton gin

While the North industrialized, the South remained agricultural.

now Southern lands had become available all the way to the Mississippi and the Sabine River.

The balance between North and South in regard to slavery that existed at the time of the constitution continued to exist, at least on the surface, until 1820. Of the 22 states in the Union in 1819, 11 were slave states and 11 committed to freedom. But now the Missouri territory had gained sufficient population to be admitted into the Union as a state. As her settlers had mostly come from the South, Missouri was expected to become a slave state, as had happened in Alabama in 1819. Congress was sharply divided on this issue and a long, bitter debate followed, until a compromise was achieved: Missouri was admitted as a slave state, but Maine, certainly a free one, was to be admitted also, preserving the balance and with the proviso[4] that in the future the territory acquired through the Louisiana Purchase (west of the Mississippi), slavery north of the southern boundary of Missouri (latitude 36° 30′) would be prohibited.

The population difference between North and South had also changed drastically during this time. While the South stayed with large plantation-type agriculture, the North industrialized and expanded rapidly into the Western territories. By 1830, one million more lived in the free states than in the slave states, and by 1840 the difference was almost two million. The South had reason to be worried: The tariff legislation had shown that the North could outvote the South in the House of Representatives; internationally the institution of slavery was disappearing fast. The new states of South America, which had fought for their independence against Spain in the 1820s, abolished slavery immediately—Mexico, the last one, in 1829. In the British

4 **proviso:** stipulation; a clause in a contract

empire, slavery was finally stopped by the Abolition Act of 1833, and in the United States, propaganda against the institution on moral grounds, which had existed almost from the beginning, became stronger and louder.

All in all, in spite of constant friction, the balance between North and South was preserved in the late 1830s and early 1840s. When, in 1836, Arkansas was admitted to the Union as a slave state, Michigan followed the next year as a free one, and the same process took place when slaveholding Florida became a state in 1845, with free Iowa following in 1846. One constant source of mutual irritation, however, was the situation of fugitive slaves. The Constitution had given slaveholders the right to recover slaves if they escaped to another, presumably Northern, state. But the activity of the abolitionists[5] and the increasing hostility of the people in the North made such recovery more and more difficult. When, in 1842, the U. S. Supreme Court declared a Pennsylvania state law that forbade the seizure of fugitive slaves unconstitutional, there was indignation in the North. The enforcement of these laws remained lax, however, and a regular "underground railroad" system was developed by white and free black abolitionists in the North to help fugitives escape into safe Northern states or Canada. Many Northern statesmen, such as William H. Seward of New York and Charles Sumner of Massachusetts, argued eloquently that slavery was morally wrong and ought to be abolished.

Harriet Tubman, who helped slaves escape via the Underground Railroad.

Meanwhile, the general attitude of Southerners also had stiffened. While most of the early statesmen from Virginia, like Washington and Jefferson, had deplored the system, people now accepted it as right and desirable. The inferiority of the black race was derived from the Bible (the "graceless sons of Ham").[6] As the number of blacks increased, the fear of uprisings, such as had been attempted by Nat Turner[7] and others,

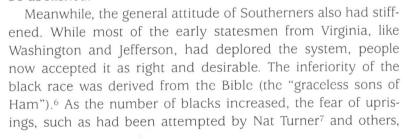

5 **abolitionists:** those who actively condemned slavery

6 **sons of Ham:** In the Bible, Ham was one of Noah's sons. Ham's children were said to have dark skin.

7 **Nat Turner:** a slave and preacher who led a slave revolt in Virginia in 1831. Turner and about 60 others killed about 60 whites before the Virginia militia stopped them. Turner was hanged.

grew and, with it, the resentment of the support and sympathy the slaves received in the Northern states. More and more, the Southerners saw themselves as one social unit, and insisted that the property of slaveowners was protected by the Constitution throughout the Union.

In spite of the cotton boom, slavery was not enriching the South. The slaves were kept ignorant and received no reward for their labor, and therefore, quite naturally, worked as little as they could, having nothing to gain by industry. There was waste everywhere, and the economy, which was concentrated in cotton, rice, tobacco and sugar had become stagnant. Meanwhile, the Northern states engaged in a great variety of enterprises and expanded rapidly, both in population and in territory. The North also found a great market for its goods in the Southern states, so the industry bosses and prominent bankers were interested in maintaining peace and the status quo.[8]

The only way that the Southern slave states could hope to keep abreast with the Northwestern expansion of the free states was to make Texas a part of the United States and reintroduce slavery there.

For a long time the slavery issue had been discussed mainly in Congress and in the hundreds of newspapers that appeared all over the country. It was now, all of a sudden, debated in thousands of households, in the North as well as in the South, because of one book that, shortly after its appearance in 1851, was more widely read throughout the world than any other: Harriet Beecher Stowe's *Uncle Tom's Cabin*. Although hardly a literary masterpiece, the book vividly described the conditions of slavery in the South, the misery of the slaves and the cruelty of the slaveowners. Read by hundreds of thousands of Americans, it did more to arouse sympathies for the enslaved than any other single factor. In the South, the book was decried as unfair, one-sided and essentially incorrect. In the North, the image of the villain Simon Legree became the prototype of the typical Southern slavemaster. The South began to see a wild abolitionist in every Northerner.

Harriet Beecher Stowe

135,000 SETS, 270,000 VOLUMES SOLD.

UNCLE TOM'S CABIN

FOR SALE HERE.

The Greatest Book of the Age.

| 8 **status quo:** current state of affairs

Still, the peace achieved by the 1850 compromise[9] could have continued under the Democrats after the victory of their presidential candidate, Franklin Pierce, in the 1852 election. In retrospect, it seems that the issue of slavery in the new territories may have subsided slowly had it been left alone. But Stephen A. Douglas, Democratic senator from Illinois, proposed a new settlement for the Northwest territories, which has been called the most fateful legislation in all American history, the so-called Kansas-Nebraska Act. By this expansion of the principle of Popular Sovereignty (or "squatter sovereignty," as it was called by its opponents), Douglas hoped to reunite the badly split Southern and Northern wings of the Democratic Party and open the way for a trans-continental railway through the Northern territories. But the acceptance of the Act in 1854 had a number of unforeseen results. Since the territory involved lay north of latitude 36° 30', the old Missouri Compromise of 1820 was thereby definitely repealed[10]—though some claimed that this had been done already by the compromise of 1850. It destroyed the three-year truce, split the Democratic Party worse than ever, meant practically the end of the Whig Party, started a new political party and instigated what amounted to a civil war in Kansas. The chances of avoiding a civil war had been fair before Kansas-Nebraska; after it was enacted, they were slim indeed.

ORDER NO.11, MARTIAL LAW 1869–7 George Caleb Bingham

9 **1850 compromise:** Developed by Henry Clay, this settlement allowed Califonia to enter as a free state; New Mexico and Arizona were organized as territories, and the residents of those territories would vote to decide if slavery would be allowed.

10 **repealed:** abandoned

PRE WAR EVENTS
UP TO 1860

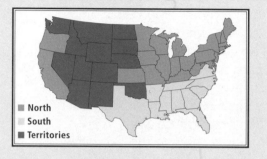

North
South
Territories

1808
U.S. outlaws slave trade with other countries, though U.S. slaveowners may still trade among themselves

1831
Slave Nat Turner leads uprising; 57 whites killed; Turner and accomplices executed (Virginia).

South passes harsh laws to control slaves

1837
Abolitionist newspaperman Elijah Lovejoy killed by pro-slavery mob (Illinois)

1820
Missouri Compromise sets precedent for states' rights on slavery issue: Missouri becomes slave state and Maine declared free state

Liberia established on West African coast for freed slaves

1834
Freed slave Denmark Vesey executed for plotting slave uprising (South Carolina)

1845
Escaped slave Frederick Douglass publishes his autobiography

1852

Author Harriet Beecher Stowe releases her book *Uncle Tom's Cabin* showing harshness of slavery

1849

Slave Harriet Tubman escapes and leads other escapees to freedom by the Underground Railroad

1856

Lawrence, Kansas, destroyed by proslavery activists. State government splits, one proslavery and one antislavery.

1859

Abolitionist John Brown leads raid at Harper's Ferry (Virginia) with plans to arm slaves and revolt. Brown is executed for treason.

1850

Compromise of 1850 written; California enters Union as free state; Utah and New Mexico territories undecided

Stronger fugitive slave law enacted

1854

Kansas-Nebraska Act passed; each territory votes on slave or free position. Kansas civil war begins, as proslavery and antislavery forces battle to control state government.

1857

Dred Scott decision rules that slaves have no civil rights under U.S. law.

1860

November
Abraham Lincoln elected President

December
South Carolina secedes

$200 REWARD!

Ran away from his owner [a Lady residing near Upper Marlboro, Prince George's County, Md.] on or about the 12th inst. of this month, a bright Mulatto man named Frank, a carpenter by trade, he is about five feet 9 or 10 inches high, light grey eyes, slow in speech, and very good personal appearance, about twenty-five years of age, his clothing good.

One Hundred dollars will be paid if apprehended within thirty miles of home, if more than thirty, the above reward, provided he be secured in Jail so that his owner gets him again.

W. D. BOWIE,
for the owner,
Buena Vista Post Office, Prince George's Co., Md.
February 14th, 1853.

SHORT STOR

EVENTS OF THE WAR
1861 – 1865

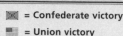

ILLINOIS

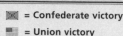 = Confederate victory

= Union victory

KANSAS

MISSOURI

1863

May
Battle of Chancellorsville (Virginia)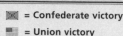

Confederate General "Stonewall" Jackson accidentally shot by own troops; dies six days later

July
Battle of Gettysburg (Pennsylvania); losses great on both sides;
Union General Grant's siege of Vicksburg, Mississippi, ends, Union now controls entire Mississippi River, cutting Confederacy in two

August
Missouri Confederate guerrilla William Quantrill and raiders attack Lawrence, Kansas, brutally butchering nearly 200 civilians

September
Battle of Chickamauga (Tennessee)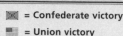

November
Gettysburg Address commemorates deaths (Pennsylvania)

Battle at Chattanooga (Tennessee)

1861

January
Mississippi, Florida, Alabama, Georgia, and Louisiana secede

February
Texas secedes

April
1st major Battle at Fort Sumter (South Carolina)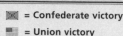

May
Arkansas, North Carolina, Virginia secede

St. Louis Riots begin four years of guerrilla warfare (Missouri)

July
First Battle of Bull Run or Manassas (Virginia)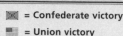

Robert E. Lee

Ulysses S. Grant

1862

ARKANSAS

MISSISSIPPI

March
Union ironclad *Monitor* vs. Confederate *Merrimack* (Louisiana)

April
Battle of Shiloh (Tennessee); one of bloodiest battles of war

New Orleans captured

June/July
Battle of Seven Days (Virginia)

August
Second Battle of Bull Run or Manassas (Virginia)

LOUISIANA

September
Battle of Antietam (Maryland); bloodiest day of war

Emancipation Proclamation frees all slaves as of January 1, 1863

New Orleans

PENNSYLVANIA

NEW JERSEY

☀ Gettysburg

☀ Antietam

OHIO

MARYLAND

DELAWARE

Shenandoah Valley

☀ First Bull Run

☀ Second Bull Run

INDIANA

☀ Chancellorsville

Wilderness ☀

WEST VIRGINIA

☀ Spotsylvania

Appomattox
Court House

☀ Richmond

KENTUCKY

VIRGINIA

1865

NORTH CAROLINA

January
Missouri slaves freed

13th Amendment abolishes slavery of any form

February
Union forces raise U.S. flag at Fort Sumter (South Carolina) 🏳️

April
Confederate General Lee surrenders to Union General Grant at Appomattox Court House (Virginia) 🏳️

President Lincoln shot by John Wilkes Booth at Ford's Theater (Washington, D.C.); dies next day

Vice President Andrew Johnson sworn in as President

Confederate General Joseph Johnson surrenders to Union General Sherman 🏳️

John Wilkes Booth captured and shot by Federal cavalry; dies next day

May
Skirmish between Union and Confederate forces at Palmitto Ranch (Texas); officially last battle of Civil War with ironic Confederate win

SOUTH CAROLINA

☀ Fort Sumter

**John
Wilkes
Booth**

TENNESSEE

Chattanooga ☀

Atlanta ☀

ALABAMA

1864

GEORGIA

May
Battle of the Wilderness (Virginia)

Battle of Spotsylvania Court House (Virginia) 🏴

June
Battle in English Channel; Confederate warship *Alabama* sunk 🏳️

September
Union General Sherman occupies Atlanta (Georgia) 🏳️

Battle in Shenandoah Valley (Virginia) 🏳️

November
President Lincoln re-elected

General Sherman begins March to the Sea (Georgia)

**William
Tecumseh Sherman**

FLORIDA

CONCEPT VOCABULARY

You will find the following terms and definitions useful as you read and discuss the selections in this book.

abolitionist one who fought against slavery

armory/arsenal a place where guns and ammunition are stored or manufactured

artillery large, mounted guns, such as cannons and howitzers; members of the army who use such weapons

conscription/draft required enrollment into the military

Confederacy (Confederate States of America/CSA) the alliance of 11 Southern states that withdrew from the United States after 1860. The states were Alabama, Arkansas, Florida, Georgia, Louisiana, Mississippi, North Carolina, South Carolina, Tennessee, Texas, and Virginia.

Democrats members of a political party which promoted letting settlers in new territories decide for themselves the issue of slavery. This stand deeply divided the party in 1860, and two separate candidates for president were nominated, Stephen A. Douglas for the Northern faction and John C. Breckenridge for the Southern faction.

dysentery severe diarrhea; cause of the majority of deaths in the Civil War

emancipation to free from the control of another; here, it refers to the movement to free the slaves

Federal anything having to do with the government of the United States of America

Reconstruction the readmission of the 11 Southern states which seceded into the United States after the Civil War

Republicans members of a political party founded before the Civil War. Many of its members opposed slavery.

secession withdrawal from an organization or political union

siege a military blockade of a city to force it to surrender

States' Rights a belief that all power not specifically given to the Federal government belongs to the states. For example, the U.S. Constitution does not say how students are to be taught, so States' Rights advocates believe only the states should determine how students are taught.

Union another name for the United States of America during the Civil War

zealot a member of a group with great devotion to a cause

CLUSTER ONE

1861-1862: WHAT WERE THEY FIGHTING FOR?

Thinking Skill ANALYZING

Confederate volunteers before the
Battle of First Bull Run, 1861.

Confederate troops fire at Fort Sumter.

FORT SUMTER FALLS

excerpt from *A Wartime Journal*

MARY BOYKIN CHESNUT

South Carolina seceded from the Union shortly after Lincoln's election in 1860. The state insisted it owned the three federal forts in Charleston's harbor—Fort Moultrie, Castle Pickney, and Fort Sumter. U.S. Army Major Robert Anderson was in charge of Fort Moultrie and soon moved his soldiers to the incomplete Fort Sumter because it was easier to defend. South Carolina's leaders saw this as a threat. Soon the state militia occupied the other forts and began to prepare an attack on Fort Sumter. Mary Boykin Chesnut was a member of South Carolina's political society. Her husband had been a member of the U.S. Senate before he resigned to support secession. In these excerpts from her diary, she comments on the tense situation developing in Charleston Harbor.

March 1861

"Now this is positive," they say. "Fort Sumter is to be relieved, and we are to have no war."

If there be no war, how triumphant Mr. Chesnut will be. He is the only man who has persisted from the first that this would be a *peaceful* revolution. Heaven grant it may prove so.

April 7, 1861

Things are happening so fast.

My husband has been made an aide-de-camp[1] of General Beauregard.

1 **aide-de-camp:** an officer who serves as an assistant

Three hours ago we were quietly packing to go home. The convention has adjourned.

Now he tells me the attack upon Fort Sumter may begin tonight. Depends upon Anderson and the fleet outside. The *Herald* says that this show of war outside of the bar is intended for Texas.[2]

John Manning came in with his sword and red sash. Pleased as a boy to be on Beauregard's staff while the row goes on. He has gone with Wigfall to Captain Hartstene with instructions.

Mr. Chestnut is finishing a report he had to make to the convention.

Mrs. Hayne called. She had, she said, "but one feeling, pity for those who are not here."

Jack Preston, Willie Alston—"the take-life-easys," as they are called—with John Green, "the big brave," have gone down to the island—volunteered as privates.

General James Chesnut and wife, Mary

Seven hundred men were sent over. Ammunition wagons rumbling along the streets all night. Anderson burning blue lights—signs and signals for the fleet outside, I suppose.

Today at dinner there was no allusion to things as they stand in Charleston Harbor. There was an undercurrent of intense excitement. There could not have been a more brilliant circle. In addition to our usual quartet (Judge Withers, Langdon Cheves, and Trescot) our two governors dined with us, Means and Manning.

These men all talked so delightfully. For once in my life I listened.

That over, business began. In earnest, Governor Means rummaged a sword and red sash from somewhere and brought it for Colonel Chesnut, who has gone to demand the surrender of Fort Sumter.

2 **this show of war outside of the bar is intended for Texas:** Chesnut is noting that South Carolina felt it had to attack Fort Sumter to encourage Texas to join the Confederacy.

And now, patience—we must wait.

Why did that green goose Anderson go into Fort Sumter? Then everything began to go wrong.

Now they have intercepted a letter from him, urging them to let him surrender. He paints the horrors likely to ensue if they will not.

He ought to have thought of all that before he put his head in the hole.

April 12, 1861

Anderson will not capitulate.

Yesterday was the merriest, maddest dinner we have had yet. Men were more audaciously wise and witty. We had an unspoken foreboding it was to be our last pleasant meeting. Mr. Miles dined with us today. Mrs. Henry King rushed in: "The news, I come for the latest news—all of the men of the King family are on the island"—of which fact she seemed proud.

While she was here, our peace negotiator—or envoy—came in. That is, Mr. Chesnut returned—his interview with Colonel Anderson had been deeply interesting—but was not inclined to be communicative, wanted his dinner. Felt for Anderson. Had telegraphed to President Davis for instructions.

What answer to give Anderson, etc., etc. He has gone back to Fort Sumter with additional instructions.

I do not pretend to go to sleep. How can I? If Anderson does not accept terms—at four—the orders are—he shall be fired upon.

I count four—St. Michael chimes. I begin to hope. At half-past four, the heavy booming of a cannon.

I sprang out of bed. And on my knees—prostrate—I prayed as I never prayed before.

There was a sound of stir all over the house—pattering of feet in the corridor—all seemed hurrying one way. I put on my double gown and a shawl and went too. It was to the housetop.

The shells were bursting. In the dark I heard a man say, "waste of ammunition."

I knew my husband was rowing about in a boat somewhere in that dark bay. And that the shells were roofing it over—bursting toward the fort. If Anderson was obstinate—he was to order the forts on our side to open fire. Certainly fire had begun. The regular roar of the cannon—

there it was. And who could tell what each volley accomplished of death and destruction.

The women were wild, there on the housetop. Prayers from the women and imprecations from the men, and then a shell would light up the scene. Tonight, they say, the forces are to attempt to land. The *Harriet Lane* had her wheelhouse[3] smashed and put back to sea.

We watched up there—everybody wondered. Fort Sumter did not fire a shot.

Today Miles and Manning, colonels now—aides to Beauregard—dined with us. The latter hoped I would keep the peace. I give him only good words, for he was to be under fire all day and night, in the bay carrying orders, etc.

Last night—or this morning truly—up on the housetop I was so weak and weary I sat down on something that looked like a black stool. "Get up, you foolish woman—your dress is on fire," cried a man. And he put me out. It was a chimney, and the sparks caught my clothes. Susan Preston and Mr. Venable then came up. But my fire had been extinguished before it broke into a regular blaze.

Do you know, after all that noise and our tears and prayers, nobody has been hurt. Sound and fury, signifying nothing.[4] A delusion and a snare . . . .

April 13, 1861

Nobody hurt, after all. How gay we were last night.

Reaction after the dread of all the slaughter we thought those dreadful cannons were making such a noise in doing.

Not even a battery the worse for wear.

Fort Sumter has been on fire. He has not yet silenced any of our guns. So the aides—still with swords and red sashes by way of uniform—tell us.

But the sound of those guns makes regular meals impossible. None of us go to table. But tea trays pervade the corridors, going everywhere.

---

3 **wheelhouse:** enclosed area on the deck of a ship that shelters the steering equipment and the pilot.

4 **sound and fury, signifying nothing:** a quote from Shakespeare's Macbeth.

Some of the anxious hearts lie on their beds and moan in solitary misery. Mrs. Wigfall and I solace ourselves with tea in my room.

These women have all a satisfying faith. . . .

But our men could not tarry with us in these cool shades and comfortable quarters—water unlimited, excellent table, etc., etc. They have gone back to Manassas,[5] and the faithful Brewster with them, to bring us the latest news. They left us in excellent spirits, which we shared until they were out of sight. We went with them to Warrenton and there heard that General Johnston was in full retreat and that a column was advancing upon Beauregard.

So we came back, all forlorn. If our husbands are taken prisoners, what will they do with them? . . .

Lincoln wants four hundred millions of money—and men in proportion. Can he get them?

He will find us a heavy handful.

---

5 **Manassas:** city in Northern Virginia. It was later the site of two Civil War battles.

Field Notes

Battle: Fort Sumter

Location: Charleston Harbor, South Carolina

Date: April 12, 1861

Commanding Officers:

 Confederate P.T.G. Beauregard

 Union Major Robert Anderson

Behind the lines: Anderson had asked to fire a final salute when the U.S. Flag was lowered. One soldier was killed during that salute, the first official casualty of the Civil War.

Winner: Confederacy

Union soliders make a meal of hardtack, a tough cracker-like
food made of unleavened flour.

REFLECTIONS ON
THE CIVIL WAR

Many in the Union and the Confederacy thought the war would be over quickly. Young men joined the armies of both sides for adventure, to uphold family honor, or simply for the money. As Catton shows, Army life was not what they expected.

In the Civil War, the common soldiers of both sides were the same sort of people: untrained and untaught young men, mostly from the country. There weren't many cities then, and they weren't very large, so the average soldier generally came either from a farm or from some very small town or rural area. He had never been anywhere; he was completely unsophisticated. He joined up because he wanted to, because his patriotism had been aroused. The bands were playing, the recruiting officers were making speeches, so he got stirred up and enlisted. Sometimes, he was not altogether dry behind the ears.

When the boy joined the army, he would, of course, be issued clothing. He would get his uniform—pants, coat, shoes, and underwear. In the frontier regions, the quartermasters discovered that quite a lot of these young men picked up the underwear and looked at it and said, "What is this?" They had never seen any before. They hadn't worn it back home. Well, they caught on. They were fresh out of the backwoods, most of them.

The boys from the country and the very small towns seemed to have made better soldiers than the boys from the cities. In the North, for instance, the boys from the rural areas, and especially from the Middle

West, which they then called the Northwest, were a little tougher than the boys from the big cities. They could stand more; they were more self-reliant; perhaps they were more used to handling weapons. In any case, they made very good soldiers. On the Southern side, the same was true—even more so. A larger percentage of the men came from rural areas because there were fewer cities in the South. A number of them didn't even bother with shoes, but they were very, very bad boys to get into a fight with.

The war was greeted in its first few weeks almost as a festival. Everybody seemed relieved. People went out and celebrated, both in the North and in the South. There were parades, bands playing, flags flying; people seemed almost happy. Large numbers of troops were enlisted; as a matter of fact, again in both the North and the South, more men offered themselves than could be handled. Neither the Union nor the Confederate government had the weapons, uniforms, or anything else to equip all of the men who tried to enlist.

Both armies contained a number of very ardent teenagers who had lied about their age in order to get into the army in the first place. Legal age, of course, was eighteen. It turned out that, in the North at least, a very common little gag had been developed. A boy who was under eighteen and wanted to enlist would take a piece of paper and scribble the figure eighteen on it. Then he would take off his shoe, placing the piece of paper into the sole of his shoe, put it back on and tie it up. He would go to the recruiting station, and since he would obviously be looking rather young, sooner or later the recruiting officer would look at him and say, "How old are you, son?" The boy, in perfect honesty, could say, "I am over eighteen."

The point about that is not so much that young men were lying about their age in order to get into the army but that they would go to the trouble of working out a gag like that. A man simply wouldn't dream of taking an oath that he was eighteen when he wasn't. Lying to the government was a little beyond him, but he would work out a thing like this and could say honestly, "I'm over eighteen," and that made it quite all right.

A set of statistics were compiled about the average Northern soldier that are rather interesting. They apply pretty much to the South as well. An average soldier was 5 feet 8 1/4 inches tall; he weighed just over 143 pounds. Forty-eight percent were farmers, 24 percent were mechanics, 15 percent were laborers, 5 percent were businessmen, and 3 percent were professional men. That was really a kind of cross-section of the population of the United States at that time: about one-half farmers, about 40 percent working men, and 10 percent businessmen or professionals.

When a man joined the Union army, he was given shoes that must have been a little bit of a trial to wear. In a great many cases, army contractors simply made the right and left shoes identical. They were squared off at the toe, and it didn't matter which one you put on which foot; they were supposed to work either way. They must have been very uncomfortable, and I imagine they account for a great many of the cases of footsore soldiers who fell out on the march and stumbled into camp long after everybody else had gone to bed.

The Civil War soldier, on the Northern side at least, got a great deal to eat; the trouble was that most of it was not very good. The Union army enlisted no cooks or bakers during the entire war.

Originally, each man was supposed to cook for himself. It happened, of course, practically immediately that company kitchens were established. Men were detailed from the ranks to act as cooks; some of them cooked fairly well, and some of them, of course, cooked abominably. But whatever they cooked, the boys ate.

The basic ration for the Civil War soldier, particularly on the march, where it was not possible to carry along vegetables, was salt pork or bacon and hardtack. The hardtack was a big soda cracker, quite thick and, as the name implies, very tough—made tough so that it wouldn't fall into pieces while it was joggling around in a man's haversack.[1] When the hardtack was fresh, it was apparently quite good to eat. The trouble is that it was very rarely fresh. Boxes of hardtack would sit on railroad platforms or sidetracked in front of warehouses for weeks and months at a time, and by the time the soldier got them, they were often infested and not very good.

[1] **haversack:** similar to a backpack; used to carry supplies and personal belongings

Every soldier carried some sort of a tin can in which he could boil coffee. Coffee was issued in the whole bean, for when the government issued ground coffee, they could never quite trust the contractors not to adulterate it. When the soldier made coffee, he would put a handful of beans in a bucket and grind them with the butt of his musket. In the morning, in camp, you could tell when the boys were getting up by the rhythmic clinking, grinding noise that came up from in front of every tent.

The soldier also had sugar to go with his coffee, and he would boil his coffee in his little tin can and then dump in some sugar. He would usually have a skillet in which to fry his bacon. Sometimes he would crumble up hardtack and drop the crumbs in the sizzling bacon fat and make a rather indescribable mess—I guess a healthy young man who got a good deal of exercise could digest it without too much difficulty.

In the Civil War, which lasted four years, about 600,000 young Americans, North and South together, lost their lives. That is not the total casualty list; it is the number that actually went under the sod.[2] The wounded, the missing, the prisoners, were in another list. Six hundred thousand is the number of lives that were actually lost.

If you want to understand what a terrible drain that was on the country, reflect that the total population in the United States in the 1860s was about an eighth or a ninth of what it is today. The number of men killed in that war, if you interpret it in today's terms, would come to something between four and four and one-half million. In other words, a perfectly frightful toll of American lives was taken.

There are a good many reasons why the toll was so high. More than one-half of the men who died were not killed in action; they simply died of camp diseases: typhoid fever, pneumonia, dysentery, and childhood diseases like measles and chicken pox.

To begin with, medical science then was woefully inadequate. Doctors simply did not know what caused such devastating camp diseases as typhoid fever, which accounted for about one-fourth of all deaths in army hospitals. Malaria, a plague of the Virginia swamp country, was attributed to "miasmic vapors" arising from stagnant waters and not to the pestifer-ous mosquitoes bred therein. (The vapors were also largely blamed for typhoid and dysentery.) Nothing was known about how and why wounds became infected, and so nothing much was done to prevent infection;

2 **went under the sod:** died

surgeons talked soberly about "laudable pus" which was expected to appear a few days after an operation or a gunshot wound, its laudable character arising because it showed that the body was discharging poisons.

The number of men who simply got sick and died, or who got a minor scratch or cut and then could do nothing to check the infection, was appalling. Just to be in the army in the 1860s was much more dangerous than anything we know about today, even though many a man in the army never got into action. It was a very common thing—in fact, almost the rule—for a Civil War regiment on either side to lose about half of its strength in men who either became sick or died or became so ill they had to get medical discharges before the regiment ever saw action. Whereas a Civil War regiment, on paper, contained about one thousand men, in actual fact, a regiment that went into battle with as many as five hundred men was quite fortunate.

Not long after the war began, whenever a Northern army and a Southern army were camped fairly close to each other, the men on the picket lines[3] would get acquainted with one another and would call little informal truces. The Northern soldiers would bring in coffee to trade. Along the Rappahannock River, they made quite a thing of constructing little toy boats out of planks. A boat would be maybe two feet long, with a mast and a sail. Loaded with coffee, it would be sent out into the stream, pointed south, and when it would get across the river, the Confederate soldiers would unload the coffee, stock it with tobacco, and send it back.

This led to some rather odd happenings, since men who are stopping to trade with each other are apt to get a little friendly along the way. There was one rather famous occasion, again along the Rappahannock River, when in a building not far behind the Confederate lines back of the outposts, there was going to be a dance one evening, and the Confederate pickets invited their Yankee friends to come over and go to the dance.

Half a dozen Yankee soldiers, leaving their guns behind them, crossed the river in the darkness, went to the dance, and had a very good time— until a Confederate officer appeared just when the festivities were at their height. He was, of course, horrified and ordered the Yankee soldiers arrested and thrown into prison, at which point the Confederates begged

---

3 **picket lines:** groups of soldiers posted around camps
to guard against attack

him not to do this. They said they had given the Yankees their word that everything would be all right if they came to the dance, and asked that the officer let them go.

Well, the officer saw some point to that appeal. He couldn't violate or cause his men to violate their honor, so after giving all hands a don't-let-it-happen-again lecture, he released the Yankee prisoners, and they went home, with a good dance under their belts.

Along the Rapidan River during the winter of 1863 and 1864, the armies for a number of miles had outposts that were drawn up very close to each other. In fact, in one or two places, they actually overlapped. The Yankees had a way of advancing their picket lines in the night and pulling them back in the daytime. The Confederates did it just the other way around; their picket lines were a little farther forward by day than by night. Pretty soon it turned out that there was a picket post, with a log cabin and a fireplace, that was used at night by the Yankees and in the daytime by the Confederates. The boys worked out a deal: each party would leave a stack of firewood on hand and be sure to get out before the other one got there. They kept on that way quite pleasantly for some months.

At the great Battle of Fredericksburg, down at the far end of the line where the fighting was not very heavy, there was a woodland stretch held by the Confederates on one side and the Yankees on the other. The pickets, again, were quite close together, and the skirmish lines[4] not much farther apart. The men got to catcalling and jeering at each other and making insulting remarks. This went on for quite a while in much the same way that a couple of high school football cheering sections might yell back and forth at each other. Finally, a couple of soldiers, a Confederate and a Yankee, got really angry. They got so angry that they had to have a fight. So all along the line in this particular section of the woodland, the soldiers called an informal truce, and the riled-up Yankee and Southerner got out and had a very fine, soul-satisfying fistfight. I don't know who came out on top, but at last the fight ended, as all such fights do, and the men went to a nearby stream and washed the blood off their faces and shook hands. Then both sides went back, picked up their weapons, and started shooting at each other again.

It was that kind of a war—rather informal, and fought between men who, when left alone, got along together beautifully. You've often heard

4 **skirmish lines:** point at which opposing troops meet and fight

it spoken of as the War Between Brothers. Actually, it really was that.

The siege of Vicksburg was another case where the picket lines were so close together that on one occasion the Southerners and the Northerners had a little meeting and came to an agreement as to just where the picket lines ought to go, so they wouldn't trespass on each other's territory.

During this siege, one of the Confederates out on the picket line asked if there were any Missouri regiments in the army immediately opposing his section. He was a Missourian himself and was looking for his brother. The Yankees made inquiry, and pretty soon they came forward with the Confederate soldier's brother—both boys from Missouri, one of them in Confederate gray and the other in Federal blue. The Confederate had a roll of bills in his hand and gave them to his brother to send to their mother, who was peaceably at home in Missouri. He couldn't get things out from Vicksburg through the Union lines, Vicksburg being completely surrounded, so he asked his brother to send them to her, and the brother did. There was no shooting while these arrangements were made, then the brothers shook hands and retired to their individual lines, and the shooting started up again.

During the fighting at Crampton's Gap in Maryland in the fall of 1862, the Confederates were slowly withdrawing. They were fighting a rear-guard action rather than a regular battle. One Yankee soldier got a little too far forward, slipped, and accidentally slid down the side of the steep hill on which he had been posted, winding up at the bottom of the hill in a thicket. There he confronted a Confederate soldier who wasn't ready to retreat yet. The two men grabbed their guns. But eventually they figured there was no point in shooting each other here, off in a quiet corner where there wasn't much going on, so they laid down their weapons and made an agreement. They would stay where they were with no shooting. At the end of the day if the Confederates had advanced, the Yankee would be the Confederate soldier's prisoner. If the Yankees had advanced, then the Confederate would be the Yankee's prisoner. Meanwhile, there wasn't any sense in getting shot. The Confederates eventually withdrew, and the Yankee soldier found he had taken a prisoner.

One of the most touching stories I know involving this acquaintanceship—friendship, really—between the rival soldiers took place at Fredericksburg, Virginia, along the Rappahannock, a couple of months after the big battle there. The Rappahannock River is not very wide, and the men on the northern bank could easily talk with the men on the southern bank if they raised their voices a little. One winter afternoon when nothing much was going on, a number of the Federal army bands were massed on the hillside overlooking the river valley to give a little informal concert. They played all of the Northern patriotic songs, and the Northern soldiers crowded around to listen. On the opposite shore, the Confederate soldiers gathered to enjoy the concert.

After a while, the band had pretty well run through its repertoire, and there was a pause, whereupon some of the Confederates shouted, "Now play some of ours." So the band began to play Southern tunes. They played "Dixie" and "Bonnie Blue Flag" and "Yellow Rose of Texas" and I don't know what all. They played Southern tunes while the Southern and Northern armies sat in the quiet and listened.

It was getting on toward dusk by this time, so the band, to signal the end of the concert, went into "Home, Sweet Home." Both armies together tried to sing it, and it was rather a sentimental occasion. After all, these boys were a long way from home. They knew perfectly well that a great many of them were never going to see home again; as soon as the warm weather came, they would be fighting each other. The song got to be a little too much for them, and pretty soon they choked up and couldn't sing, and the band finished the music all by itself.

A couple of months later, the troops faced each other in the terrible Battle of Chancellorsville. ▌

Eighth New York State Militia, 1861.

THE PICKETS

ROBERT W. CHAMBERS

Hi Yank!"

"Shut up!" replied Alden, wriggling to the edge of the rifle-pit. Connor also crawled a little higher and squinted through the chinks of the pine logs.

"Hey, Johnny!" he called across the river, "are you that clay-eatin' Cracker with green lamps on your pilot?"

"O Yank! Are yew the U.S. mewl with a C.S.A. brand on yewr head-stall?"

"Shut up!" replied Connor, sullenly.

A jeering laugh answered him from across the river.

"He had you there, Connor," observed Alden, with faint interest.

Connor took off his blue cap and examined the bullet-hole in the crown.

"C.S.A. brand on my head-stall, eh!" he repeated, savagely, twirling the cap between his dirty fingers.

"You called him a clay-eating Cracker," observed Alden; "and you referred to his spectacles as green lanterns on his pilot."

"I'll show him whose head-stall is branded," muttered Connor, shoving his smoky rifle through the log-crack.

Alden slid down to the bottom of the shallow pit, and watched him apathetically. He gasped once or twice, threw open his jacket at the throat, and stuffed a filthy handkerchief into the crown of his cap, arranging the ends as a shelter for his neck.

Connor lay silent, his right eye fastened upon the rifle-sight, his dusty army shoes crossed behind him. One yellow sock had slipped down over the worn shoe-heel and laid bare a dust-begrimed anklebone.

Suddenly Connor's rifle cracked; the echoes rattled and clattered away through the woods; a thin cloud of pungent vapor slowly drifted straight upward, shredding into filmy streamers among the tangled branches overhead.

"Get him?" asked Alden, after a silence.

"Nope," replied Connor. Then he addressed himself to his late target across the river:

"Hello, Johnny!"

"Hi, Yank!"

"How close?"

"Hey?"

"How close?"

"What, sonny?"

"My shot, you fool!"

"Why, sonny!" called back the Confederate, in affected surprise, "was yew a-shootin' at me?"

Bang! went Connor's rifle again. A derisive catcall answered him, and he turned furiously to Alden.

"Oh, let up," said the young fellow; "it's too hot for that."

Connor was speechless with rage, and he hastily jammed another cartridge into his long hot rifle; but Alden roused himself, brushed away a persistent fly, and crept up to the edge of the pit again.

"Hello, Johnny!" he shouted.

"That you, sonny?" replied the Confederate.

"Yes; say, Johnny, shall we call it square until four o'clock?"

"What time is it?" replied the cautious Confederate; "all our expensive gold watches is bein' repaired at Chickamauga."

At this taunt Connor showed his teeth, but Alden laid one hand on his arm and sang out: "It's two o'clock, Richmond time; Sherman has just telegraphed us from your Statehouse."

"Wall, in that case this crool war is over," replied the Confederate sharp-shooter; "we'll be easy on old Sherman."

"See here!" cried Alden; "is it a truce until four o'clock?"

"All right! Your word, Yank!"

"You have it!"

"Done!" said the Confederate, coolly rising to his feet and strolling down to the river bank, both hands in his pockets.

Alden and Connor crawled out of their ill-smelling dust-wallow, leaving their rifles behind them.

"Whew! It's hot, Johnny," said Alden, pleasantly. He pulled out a stained pipe, blew into the stem, polished the bowl with his sleeve, and sucked wistfully at the end. Then he went and sat down beside Connor, who had improvised a fishing outfit from his ramrod, a bit of string, and a rusty hook.

The Confederate rifleman also sat down on his side of the stream, puffing luxuriously on a fragrant corncob pipe. Alden watched him askance, sucking the stem of his own empty pipe. After a minute or two, Connor dug up a worm from the roots of a beech tree with his bayonet, fixed it to the hook, flung the line into the muddy current, and squatted gravely on his haunches, chewing a leaf stem.

Presently the Confederate soldier raised his head and looked across at Alden.

"What's yewr name, sonny?" he asked.

"Alden," replied the young fellow, briefly.

"Mine's Craig," observed the Confederate; "what's yewr regiment?"

"Two Hundred and Sixtieth New York; what's yours, Mr. Craig?"

"Ninety-third Maryland, *Mister* Alden."

"Quit that throwin' sticks in the water!" growled Connor. "How do you s'pose I'm goin' to catch anythin'?"

Alden tossed his stick back into the brush-heap and laughed.

"How's your tobacco, Craig?" he called out.

"Bully! How's yewr coffee 'n' tack, Alden?"

"First rate!" replied the youth.

After a silence he said, "Is it a go?"

"You bet," said Craig, fumbling in his pockets. He produced a heavy twist of Virginia tobacco, laid it on a log, hacked off about three inches with his sheath-knife, and folded it up in a big green sycamore leaf. This again he rolled into a corn-husk, weighted it with a pebble; then, stepping back, he hurled it into the air, saying, "Deal square, Yank!"

The tobacco fell at Alden's feet. He picked it up, measured it carefully with his clasp-knife, and called out: "Two and three-quarters, Craig. What do you want, hard-tack or coffee?"

"Tack," replied Craig; "don't stint!"

Alden laid out two biscuits. As he was about to hack a quarter from the third, he happened to glance over the creek at his enemy. There was no mistaking the expression in his face. Starvation was stamped on every feature.

When Craig caught Alden's eye, he spat with elaborate care, whistled a bar of the "Bonny Blue Flag," and pretended to yawn.

Alden hesitated, glanced at Connor, then placed three whole biscuits in the corn-husk, added a pinch of coffee, and tossed the parcel over to Craig.

That Craig longed to fling himself upon the food and devour it was plain to Alden, who was watching his face. But he didn't; he strolled leisurely down the bank, picked up the parcel, weighed it critically before opening it, and finally sat down to examine the contents. When he saw that the third cracker was whole and that a pinch of coffee had been added, he paused in his examination and remained motionless on the bank, head bent. Presently he looked up and asked Alden if he had made a mistake. The young fellow shook his head and drew a long puff of smoke from his pipe, watching it curl out of his nose with interest.

"Then I'm obliged to yew, Alden," said Craig; " 'low I'll eat a snack to see it ain't pizened.[1]"

He filled his lean jaws with the dry biscuit, then scooped up a tin cup full of water from the muddy river and set the rest of the cracker to soak.

"Good?" queried Alden.

"Fair," drawled Craig, bolting an unchewed segment and choking a little. "How's the twist?"

"Fine," said Alden; "tastes like stable-sweepings."

They smiled at each other across the stream.

"Sa-a-y," drawled Craig, with his mouth full, "when yew're out of twist, jest yew sing out, sonny."

"All right," replied Alden. He stretched back in the shadow of a sycamore and watched Craig with pleasant eyes.

Presently Connor had a bite and jerked his line into the air.

"Look yere," said Craig, "that ain't no way for to ketch red-horse. Yew want a ca'tridge on foh a sinker, sonny."

"What's that?" inquired Connor, suspiciously.

"Put on a sinker."

"Go on, Connor," said Alden.

Connor saw him smoking, and sniffed anxiously. Alden tossed him the twist, telling him to fill his pipe.

Presently Connor found a small pebble and improvised a sinker. He swung his line again into the muddy current, with a mechanical sidelong

---

1 **pizened:** poisoned

glance to see what Craig was doing, and settled down again on his haunches, smoking and grunting.

"Enny news, Alden?" queried Craig after a silence.

"Nothing much; except that Richmond has fallen," grinned Alden.

"Quit foolin'," urged the Southerner; "ain't there no news?"

"No. Some of our men down at Mud Pond got sick eating catfish. They caught them in the pond. It appears you Johnnys used the pond as a cemetery, and our men got sick eating the fish."

"That so?" drawled Craig; "too bad. Lots of yewr men was in Long Pond too, I reckon."

In the silence that followed two rifleshots sounded faint and dull from the distant forest.

"'Nother great Union victory," drawled Craig. "Extry! Extry! Richmond is took!"

Alden laughed and puffed his pipe.

"We licked the boots off of the 30th Texas last Monday," he said.

"Sho!" drawled Craig; "what did you go a lickin' their boots for—blackin'?"

"Oh, shut up!" said Connor from the bank; "I can't ketch no fish if you two fools don't quit jawin'."

The sun was dipping below the pine-clad ridge, flooding river and wood with a fierce radiance. The spruce needles glittered, edged with gold; every broad, green leaf wore a heart of gilded splendor, and the muddy waters of the river rolled onward like a flood of precious metal, heavy, burnished, noiseless.

From a balsam bough a thrush uttered three timid notes; a great, gauzy-winged grasshopper drifted blindly into a clump of sun-scorched weeds, click! click! cr-r-r-r!

"Purty, ain't it," said Craig, looking at the thrush. Then he swallowed the last morsel of muddy hard-tack, wiped his beard on his cuff, hitched up his trousers, took off his green glasses, and rubbed his eyes.

"A he catbird sings purtier, though," he said, with a yawn.

Alden drew out his watch, puffed once or twice, and stood up, stretching his arms in the air.

"It's four o'clock," he began, but was cut short by a shout from Connor.

"Gee whiz!" he yelled, "what have I got on this here pole?"

The ramrod was bending, the line swaying heavily in the current.

"It's four o'clock, Connor," said Alden, keeping a wary eye on Craig.

"That's all right!" called Craig; "the time's extended till yewr friend lands that there fish."

"Pulls like a porpoise," grunted Connor. "I bet it busts my ramrod!"

"Does it pull?" grinned Craig.

"Yes, a dead weight!"

"Don't it jerk kinder this way an' that," asked Craig, much interested.

"Naw," said Connor; "the bloody thing jest pulls steady."

"Then it ain't no red-horse; it's a catfish!"

"Huh!" sneered Connor; "don't I know a catfish? This ain't no catfish, lemme tell yer!"

"Then it's a log," laughed Alden.

"By gum! Here it comes," panted Connor; "here, Alden, jest you ketch it with my knife; hook the blade, blame ye!"

Alden cautiously descended the red bank of mud, holding on to roots and branches, and bent over the water. He hooked the big-bladed clasp-knife like a scythe, set the spring, and leaned out over the water.

"Now!" muttered Connor.

An oily circle appeared upon the surface of the turbid water,—another and another. A few bubbles rose and floated upon the tide.

Then something black appeared just beneath the bubbles, and Alden hooked it with his knife and dragged it shoreward. It was the sleeve of a man's coat.

Connor dropped his ramrod and gaped at the thing. Alden would have loosed it, but the knife-blade was tangled in the sleeve.

He turned a sick face up to Connor.

"Pull it in," said the older man. "Here, give it to me, lad—"

When at last the silent visitor lay upon the bank, they saw it was the body of a Union cavalryman. Alden stared at the dead face, fascinated; Connor mechanically counted the yellow chevrons upon the blue sleeve, now soaked black. The muddy water ran over the baked soil, spreading out in dust-covered pools; the spurred boots trickled slime. After a while both men turned their heads and looked at Craig. The Southerner stood silent and grave, his battered cap in his hand. They eyed each other quietly for a moment, then, with a vague gesture, the Southerner walked back into his pit and presently reappeared, trailing his rifle.

Connor had already begun to dig with his bayonet, but he glanced up sharply at the rifle in Craig's hand. Then he looked searchingly into the eyes of the Southerner. Presently he bent his head and quietly continued digging.

It was after sunset before he and Alden finished the shallow grave, Craig watching them in silence, his rifle between his knees. When they were ready they rolled the body into the hole and stood up.

Craig also rose, raising his rifle to a "present." He held it there while the two Union soldiers shoveled the earth into the grave. Then Alden went back and lifted the two rifles from the pit, handed Connor his, and waited.

"Ready!" growled Connor. "Aim!"

Alden's rifle came to his shoulder. Craig also raised his rifle.

"Fire!"

Three times the three shots rang out in the wilderness, over the unknown grave. After a moment or two Alden nodded goodnight to Craig across the river, and walked slowly toward his rifle-pit. Connor shambled after him. As he turned to lower himself into the pit he called across the river, "Good-night, Craig!"

"Good-night, Connor," said Craig.

A battle site near Gettysburg, as sketched by *Harper's Weekly* artist Alfred R. Waud, 1863.

FIRST BATTLE OF
BULL RUN

WILLIAM HOWARD RUSSELL

After the attack on Fort Sumter, Arkansas, North Carolina, and Virginia joined South Carolina, Mississippi, Alabama, Florida, Georgia, Louisiana, and Texas to form the Confederate States of America. There were a few skirmishes between the North and the South, but the first major battle was at Manassas, Virginia. The Union was overconfident and thought the Southerners would be beaten quickly. Some people from nearby Washington, D.C., even held a picnic on a hill overlooking the battlefield to watch the show. William Howard Russell, a correspondent for *The Times*, of London, England, reported on the battle's aftermath.

JULY 21, 1861

Manassas, Virginia

Centreville appeared in sight—a few houses on our front, beyond which rose a bald hill, the slopes covered with bivouac huts,[1] commissariat carts,[2] and horses, and the top crested with spectators of the fight.

The scene was so peaceful a man might well doubt the evidence of one sense that a great contest was being played out below in bloodshed. . . . But the cannon spoke out loudly from the green bushes, and the plains below were mottled, so to speak, by puffs of smoke and by white rings from bursting shells and capricious howitzers.[3] . . . With the glass I could detect now and then the flash of arms through the dust clouds

---

1 **bivouac huts:** temporary shelters
2 **commissariat carts:** supply wagons
3 **howitzers:** short cannons

GENERAL ABNER DOUBLEDAY WATCHING
HIS TROOPS CROSS THE POTOMAC
CA. 1861
David Gilmour Blythe

in the open, but no one could tell to which side the troops who were moving belonged, and I could only judge from the smoke whether the guns were fired towards or away from the hill. In the midst of our little reconnaissance Mr. Vizetelly, who has been living and, indeed, marching with one of the regiments as artist of the *Illustrated London News,* came up and told us the action had been commenced in splendid style by the Federalists,[4] who had advanced steadily, driving the Confederates before them—a part of the plan, as I firmly believe, to bring them under the range of their guns. He believed the advantages on the Federalist side were decided, though won with hard fighting.

As I turned down into the narrow road, or lane, there was a forward movement among the large four-wheeled tilt waggons, when suddenly there arose a tumult in front of me at a small bridge across the road, and then I perceived the drivers of a set of waggons with the horses turned towards me, who were endeavouring to force their way against the stream of vehicles setting in the other direction. By the side of the new set of waggons there were a number of commissariat men and soldiers, whom at first sight I took to be the baggage guard. They looked excited and alarmed and were running by the side of the horses—in front the dust quite obscured the view. At the bridge the currents met in wild disorder. "Turn back! Retreat!" shouted the men from the front, "We're whipped, we're whipped!" They cursed and tugged at the horses' heads, and struggled with frenzy to get past.

I got my horse up into the field out of the road, and went on rapidly towards the front. Soon I met soldiers who were coming through the corn, mostly without arms;[5] and presently I saw firelocks, cooking tins, knapsacks, and greatcoats on the ground, and observed that the confusion and speed of the baggage-carts became greater, and that many of them were crowded with men, or were followed by others, who clung to them. The ambulances were crowded with soldiers, but it did not look as if there were many wounded. Negro servants on led horses dashed frantically past; men in uniform, whom it were a disgrace to the profession of arms to call "soldiers," swarmed by on mules, chargers, and even draught horses, which had been cut out of carts or waggons, and went on with harness clinging to their heels, as frightened as their riders. Men literally screamed with rage and fright when their way was blocked up.

---

4 **Federalists:** soldiers fighting for the Union

5 **arms:** firearms; guns

On I rode, asking all "What is all this about?" and now and then, but rarely, receiving the answer, "We're whipped;" or, "We're repulsed." Faces black and dusty, tongues out in the heat, eyes staring—it was a most wonderful sight.

All the road from Centreville for miles presented such a sight as can only be witnessed in the track of the runaways of an utterly demoralized army. Drivers flogged, lashed, spurred, and beat their horses, or leaped down and abandoned their teams, and ran by the side of the road; mounted men, servants, and men in uniform, vehicles of all sorts, commissariat waggons thronged the narrow ways. At every shot a convulsion as it were seized upon the morbid mass of bones, sinew, wood, and iron, and thrilled through it, giving new energy and action to its desperate efforts to get free from itself. . . . The Federalists, utterly routed, had fallen back upon Arlington to defend the capital, leaving nearly five batteries of artillery, 8,000 muskets, immense quantity of stores and baggage, and their wounded and prisoners in the hands of the enemy!

Field Notes

Battle: First Bull Run/First Manassas

Location: Manassas, Virginia

Date: July 17, 1861

Commanding Officers:

  Confederate P.T.G. Beauregard

  Union Irvin McDowell

Behind the lines: Union soldiers had been fighting or marching for 14 straight hours at the battle's high point. Many dropped from exhaustion; some units became confused.

Winner: Confederacy

THE DRUMMER BOY
OF SHILOH

RAY BRADBURY

In the April night, more than once, blossoms fell from the orchard trees and lighted with rustling taps on the drumhead. At midnight a peach stone left miraculously on a branch through winter, flicked by a bird, fell swift and unseen; it struck once, like panic, and jerked the boy upright. In silence he listened to his own heart ruffle away, away—at last gone from his ears and back in his chest again.

After that he turned the drum on its side, where its great lunar face peered at him whenever he opened his eyes.

His face, alert or at rest, was solemn. It was a solemn time and a solemn night for a boy just turned fourteen in the peach orchard near Owl Creek not far from the church at Shiloh.

". . . thirty-one . . . thirty-two . . . thirty-three." Unable to see, he stopped counting.

Beyond the thirty-three familiar shadows forty thousand men, exhausted by nervous expectation and unable to sleep for romantic dreams of battles yet unfought, lay crazily askew in their uniforms. A mile farther on, another army was strewn helterskelter, turning slowly, basting themselves with the thought of what they would do when the time came—a leap, a yell, a blind plunge their strategy, raw youth their protection and benediction.

Now and again the boy heard a vast wind come up that gently stirred the air. But he knew what it was—the army here, the army there, whispering

THE HORNET'S NEST (Shiloh)   Thure de Thulstrap

to itself in the dark. Some men talking to others, others murmuring to themselves, and all so quiet it was like a natural element arisen from South or North with the motion of the earth toward dawn.

What the men whispered the boy could only guess and he guessed that it was "Me, I'm the one, I'm the one of all the rest who won't die. I'll live through it. I'll go home. The band will play. And I'll be there to hear it."

Yes, thought the boy, *that's all very well for them, they can give as good as they get!*

For with the careless bones of the young men, harvested by night and bindled around campfires, were the similarly strewn steel bones of their rifles with bayonets fixed like eternal lightning lost in the orchard grass.

Me, thought the boy, *I got only a drum, two sticks to beat it, and no shield.*

There wasn't a man-boy on this ground tonight who did not have a shield he cast, riveted, or carved himself on his way to his first attack, compounded of remote but nonetheless firm and fiery family devotion, flag-blown patriotism, and cocksure immortality strengthened by the touchstone of very real gunpowder, ramrod, Minié ball, and flint. But without these last, the boy felt his family move yet farther off in the dark, as if one of those great prairie-burning trains had chanted them away, never to return—leaving him with this drum which was worse than a toy in the game to be played tomorrow or someday much too soon.

The boy turned on his side. A moth brushed his face, but it was a peach blossom. A peach blossom flicked him, but it was a moth. Nothing stayed put. Nothing had a name. Nothing was as it once was.

If he stayed very still, when the dawn came up and the soldiers put on their bravery with their caps, perhaps they might go away, the war with them, and not notice him living small here, no more than a toy himself.

"Well, by thunder now," said a voice. The boy shut his eyes to hide inside himself, but it was too late. Someone, walking by in the night, stood over him. "Well," said the voice quietly, "here's a soldier crying *before* the fight. Good. Get it over. Won't be time once it all starts."

And the voice was about to move on when the boy, startled, touched the drum at his elbow. The man above, hearing this, stopped. The boy could feel his eyes, sense him slowly bending near. A hand must have come down out of the night, for there was a little *rat-tat* as the fingernails brushed and the man's breath fanned the boy's face.

* * *

"Why, it's the drummer boy, isn't it?"

The boy nodded, not knowing if his nod was seen. "Sir, is that you?" he said.

"I assume it is." The man's knees cracked as he bent still closer. He smelled as all fathers should smell, of salt-sweat, tobacco, horse and boot leather, and the earth he walked upon. He had many eyes. No, not eyes, brass buttons that watched the boy.

He could only be, and was, the general. "What's your name, boy?" he asked.

"Joby, sir," whispered the boy, starting to sit up.

"All right, Joby, don't stir." A hand pressed his chest gently, and the boy relaxed. "How long you been with us, Joby?"

"Three weeks, sir."

"Run off from home or join legitimate, boy?"

Silence.

"Fool question," said the general. "Do you shave yet, boy? Even more of a fool. There's your cheek, fell right off the tree overhead. And the others here, not much older. Raw, raw, the lot of you. You ready for tomorrow or the next day, Joby?"

"I think so, sir."

"You want to cry some more, go on ahead. I did the same last night."

"You, sir?"

"It's the truth. Thinking of everything ahead. Both sides figuring the other side will just give up, and soon, and the war done in weeks and us all home. Well, that's not how it's going to be. And maybe that's why I cried."

"Yes, sir," said Joby.

The general must have taken out a cigar now, for the dark was suddenly filled with the Indian smell of tobacco unlighted yet, but chewed as the man thought what next to say.

"It's going to be a crazy time," said the general. "Counting both sides, there's a hundred thousand men—give or take a few thousand—out there tonight, not one as can spit a sparrow off a tree, or knows a horse clod from a Minié ball. Stand up, bare the breast, ask to be a target, thank them and sit down, that's us, that's them. We should turn tail and train four months, they should do the same. But here we are, taken with spring fever and thinking it blood lust, taking our sulphur with cannons instead of with molasses, as it should be—going to be a hero, going to live forever. And I can see all them over there nodding agreement, save the other way around. It's wrong, boy, it's wrong as a head put on hindside front and a man marching backward through life. Sometime this week more innocents will get shot out of pure Cherokee enthusiasm than ever got shot before. Owl Creek was full of boys splashing around in the noonday sun just a few hours ago. I fear it will be full of boys again, just floating, at sundown tomorrow, not caring where the current takes them."

* * *

The general stopped and made a little pile of winter leaves and twigs in the dark as if he might at any moment strike fire to them to see his way through the coming days when the sun might not show its face because of what was happening here and just beyond.

The boy watched the hand stirring the leaves and opened his lips to say something, but did not say it. The general heard the boy's breath and spoke himself.

"Why am I telling you this? That's what you wanted to ask, eh? Well, when you got a bunch of wild horses on a loose rein somewhere, some-how you got to bring order, rein them in. These lads, fresh out of the milkshed, don't know what I know; and I can't tell them—men actually die in war. So each is his own army. I got to make one army of them. And for that, boy, I need you."

"Me!" The boy's lips barely twitched.

"You, boy," said the general quietly. "You are the heart of the army. Think about that. You are the heart of the army. Listen to me, now."

And lying there, Joby listened. And the general spoke. If he, Joby, beat slow tomorrow, the heart would beat slow in the men. They would lag by the wayside. They would drowse in the fields on their muskets. They would sleep forever after that—in those same fields, their hearts slowed by a drummer boy and stopped by enemy lead.

But if he beat a sure, steady, ever faster rhythm, then, then, their knees would come up in a long line down over that hill, one knee after the other, like a wave on the ocean shore. Had he seen the ocean ever? Seen the waves rolling in like a well-ordered cavalry charge to the sand? Well, that was it, that's what he wanted, that's what was needed. Joby was his right hand and his left. He gave the orders, but Joby set the pace.

So bring the right knee up and the right foot out and the left knee up and the left foot out, one following the other in good time, in brisk time. Move the blood up the body and make the head proud and the spine stiff and the jaw resolute. Focus the eye and set the teeth, flare the nostril and tighten the hands, put steel armor all over the men, for blood moving fast in them does indeed make men feel as if they'd put on steel. He must keep at it, at it! Long and steady, steady and long! Then, even though shot or torn, those wounds got in hot blood—in blood he'd helped stir—would feel less pain. If their blood was cold, it would be more than slaughter, it would be murderous nightmare and pain best not told and no one to guess.

The general spoke and stopped, letting his breath slack off. Then, after a moment, he said, "So there you are, that's it. Will you do that, boy? Do you know now you're general of the army when the general's left behind?"

The boy nodded mutely.

"You'll run them through for me then, boy?"

"Yes, sir."

"Good. And, maybe, many nights from tonight, many years from now, when you're as old or far much older than me, when they ask you what you did in this awful time, you will tell them—one part humble and one part proud—I was the drummer boy at the battle of Owl Creek or the Tennessee River, or maybe they'll just name it after the church there. I was the drummer boy at Shiloh. Good grief, that has a beat and sound to it fitting for Mr. Longfellow. 'I was the drummer boy at Shiloh.' Who will ever hear those words and not know you, boy, or what you thought this night, or what you'll think tomorrow or the next day when we must get up on our legs and move."

The general stood up. "Well, then. God bless you, boy. Good night."

"Good night, sir." And tobacco, brass, boot polish, salt-sweat, and leather, the man moved away through the grass.

Joby lay for a moment staring, but unable to see where the man had gone. He swallowed. He wiped his eyes. He cleared his throat. He settled himself. Then, at last, very slowly and firmly he turned the drum so it faced up toward the sky.

He lay next to it, his arm around it, feeling the tremor, the touch, the muted thunder as all the rest of the April night in the year 1862, near the Tennessee River, not far from the Owl Creek, very close to the church named Shiloh, the peach blossoms fell on the drum.

Field Notes

Battle: Shiloh/Pittsburgh Landing

Location: Pittsburgh Landing, Tennessee

Date: April 6-7, 1862

Commanding Officers:

   Confederate Albert Sidney Johnston

   Union Ulysses S. Grant

Behind the lines: Shiloh was not where Ulysses S. Grant intended to meet Confederate forces. Grant was attempting to reach Cornith, Mississippi, to control a key intersection. His army had camped near Shiloh church, in Tennessee. Confederate General Albert Sidney Johnston attacked the slumbering Union forces at 5 a.m. on April 6, 1862.

   Darkness fell just as the Confederates had beaten the Union army back to the Tennessee River. The break in fighting allowed Grant time to gather reinforcements and regroup.

Winner: Union

SHILOH *A Requiem*

(APRIL 1862)

HERMAN MELVILLE

Skimming lightly, wheeling still,
  The swallows fly low
Over the field in clouded days,
  The forest-field of Shiloh—
Over the field where April rain
Solaced the parched one stretched in pain
Through the pause of night
That followed the Sunday fight
  Around the church of Shiloh—
The church so lone, the log-built one,
That echoed to many a parting groan
    And natural prayer
  Of dying foemen mingled there—
Foemen at morn, but friends at eve—
  Fame or country least their care:
(What like a bullet can undeceive!)
  But now they lie low,
While over them the swallows skim
  And all is hushed at Shiloh.

The Colored Soldiers

Paul Laurence Dunbar

Paul Laurence Dunbar (1872-1906) was an African American
poet who often used images from the Civil War to comment about
the rise of Jim Crow laws that segregated the South after the
Civil War. Black troops were first enlisted in 1862. Fort Pillow,
near Memphis, Tennessee, is mentioned in this poem. It was
the site of an especially bloody battle that involved black
Union soldiers. At one point in the battle, Northern troops
surrendered. However, Confederates allegedly killed many of
the black troops rather than allow them to surrender.

If the muse were mine to tempt it
  And my feeble voice were strong,
If my tongue were trained to measures,
  I would sing a stirring song.
I would sing a song heroic
  Of those noble sons of Ham,
Of the gallant colored soldiers
  Who fought for Uncle Sam!

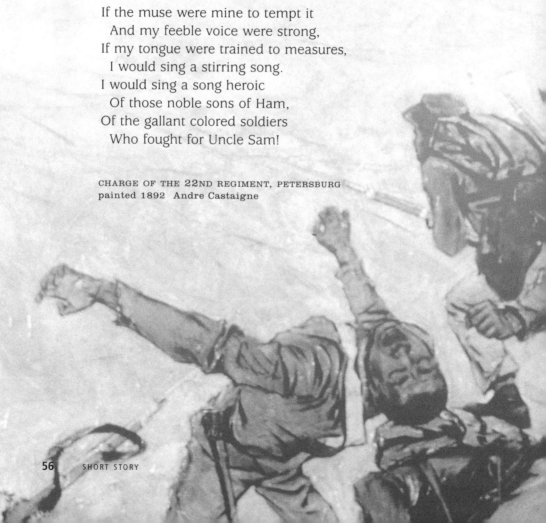

CHARGE OF THE 22ND REGIMENT, PETERSBURG
painted 1892 Andre Castaigne

In the early days you scorned them,
  And with many a flip and flout,
Said "these battles are the white man's
  And the whites will fight them out."
Up the hills you fought and faltered,
  In the vales you strove and bled,
While your ears still heard the thunder
  Of the foes' increasing tread.

Then distress fell on the nation
  And the flag was dropping low;
Should the dust pollute your banner?
  No! the nation shouted, No!
So when war, in savage triumph,
  Spread abroad his funeral pall—
Then you called the colored soldiers,
  And they answered to your call.

And like hounds unleashed and eager
  For the life blood of the prey,
Sprung they forth and bore them bravely
  In the thickest of the fray.
And where'er the fight was hottest—
  Where the bullets fastest fell,
There they pressed unblanched and fearless
  At the very mouth of hell.

Ah, they rallied to the standard
  To uphold it by their might,
None were stronger in the labors,
  None were braver in the fight.
At Forts Donelson and Henry[1]
  On the plains of Olustee,
They were foremost in the fight
  Of the battles of the free.

And at Pillow![2] God have mercy
  On the deeds committed there,
And the souls of those poor victims
  Sent to Thee without a prayer.
Let the fullness of thy pity
  O'er the hot wrought spirits sway,
Of the gallant colored soldier
  Who fell fighting on that day!

1 **Forts Donelson and Henry:** Northern victories in Tennessee where
black troops fought in 1862

2 **Pillow:** Fort Pillow, near Memphis, Tennessee, was the site of an especially
bloody battle that involved black Union soldiers in 1864.

Yes, the Blacks enjoy their freedom
  And they won it dearly, too;
For the life blood of their thousands
  Did the southern fields bedew.
In the darkness of their bondage,
  In their depths of slavery's night;
Their muskets flashed the dawning
  And they fought their way to light.

They were comrades then and brothers,
  Are they more or less to-day?
They were good to stop a bullet
  And to front the fearful fray.
They were citizens and soldiers,
  When rebellion raised its head;
And the traits that made them worthy—
  Ah! those virtues are not dead.

They have shared your nightly vigils,
  They have shared your daily toil;
And their blood with yours commingling
  Has made rich the Southern soil.
They have slept and marched and suffered
  'Neath the same dark skies as you,
They have met as fierce a foeman
  And have been as brave and true.

And their deeds shall find a record,
  In the registry of Fame;
For their blood has cleansed completely
  Every blot of Slavery's shame.
So all honor and all glory
  To those noble Sons of Ham—
To the gallant colored soldiers,
  Who fought for Uncle Sam!

RESPONDING TO CLUSTER ONE

WHAT WERE THEY FIGHTING FOR?

Thinking Skill ANALYZING

1. Mary Boykin Chesnut's diary provides a glimpse into her reactions toward the unfolding events of the Civil War. Create a chart that **analyzes** Chesnut's emotions for each entry in the excerpt of her diary on pages 23–27. You might track the following emotions on your chart: sadness, depression, anxiety, fear, excitement, etc. Be sure to include Chesnut's statement on page 5, which was written near the end of the war.

2. **Analyze** "The Pickets," "The Drummer Boy of Shiloh," and "Reflections on the Civil War." Which piece do you think is most effective in providing insights into the life of a solider?

3. **Tone** is the author's attitude toward the subject he or she is writing about. For example, a writer may express sadness or hope through a piece of writing. Review either "Shiloh" by Herman Melville or "The Colored Soldiers" by Paul Laurence Dunbar. Select two or three lines that you feel best express the tone of the poem. Be prepared to explain your choice.

4. The North and South each had their own reasons for fighting the Civil War. Using an **analysis** chart like the one below, list two or more examples from each selection that show why the North and South chose to fight.

Selection	Northern Reasons	Southern Reasons
The Civil War		
Fort Sumter Falls		
Reflections on the Civil War		

Writing Activity: Justification of War

Using the chart in question four above, write a short essay **analyzing** at least three causes that led the North and South to war. Use examples from the selections in Cluster One, the opening essay, and the timeline to support your analysis.

A Strong Analysis

- states the purpose for the analysis
- demonstrates careful examination of each part of the topic
- supports each point with evidence
- organizes information clearly
- ends with a summary of the ideas presented

CLUSTER TWO

1863: A Turning Point?

Thinking Skill COMPARING AND CONTRASTING

Guard detail of U.S. Colored Infantry
at Fort Corcoran.

FREEDOM TO SLAVES!

JAMES MCPHERSON

1st South Carolina (colored) Volunteer Regiment
celebrates Emancipation, January, 1863.

Seeing such a multitude of people in and around my church, I hurriedly sent up to the office of the first paper in which the proclamation of freedom could be printed, known as the *Evening Star*, and squeezed myself through the dense crowd that was waiting for the paper. The first sheet run off with the proclamation in it was grabbed for by three of us, but some active young man got possession of it and fled. The next sheet was grabbed for by several, and was torn into tatters. The third sheet from the press was grabbed for by several, but I succeeded in procuring so much of it as contained the proclamation, and off I went for life and death. Down Pennsylvania Avenue I ran as for my life, and when the people saw me coming with the paper in my hand they raised a shouting cheer that was almost deafening. As many as could get around me lifted me to a great platform, and I started to read the proclamation. I had run the best end of a mile, I was out of breath, and could not read. Mr. Hinton, to whom I handed the paper, read it with great force and clearness. While he was reading every kind of demonstration and gesticulation was going on. Men squealed, women fainted, dogs barked, white and colored people shook hands, songs were sung, and by this time cannons began to fire at the navy yard, and follow in the wake of the roar that had for some time been going on behind the White House. . . . Great processions of colored and white men marched to and fro and passed in front of the White House and congratulated President Lincoln on his proclamation. The President came to the window and made responsive bows, and thousands told him, if he would come out of that palace, they would hug him to death. . . . It was indeed a time of times, and nothing like it will ever be seen again in this life.

A Debt of Honor

F. Scott Fitzgerald

Prayle!"

"Here."

"Martin!"

"Absent."

"Sanderson!"

"Here."

"Carlton, for sentry duty!"

"Sick."

"Any volunteers to take his place?"

"Me, me," said Jack Sanderson, eagerly.

"All right," said the captain and went on with the roll.

It was a very cold night. Jack never quite knew how it came about. He had been wounded in the hand the day before and his gray jacket was stained a bright red where he had been hit by a stray ball. And "number six" was such a long post. From way up by the general's tent to way down by the lake. He could feel a faintness stealing over him. He was very tired and it was getting very dark—very dark.

They found him there, sound asleep, in the morning worn out by the fatigue of the march and the fight which had followed it. There was nothing the matter with him save the wounds, which were slight, and military rules were very strict. To the last day of his life Jack always remembered the sorrow in his captain's voice as he read aloud the dismal order.

Camp Bowling Green, C.S.A. Jan. 15, 1863, U.S.

For falling asleep while in a position of trust at a sentry post, private John Sanderson is hereby condemned to be shot at sunrise on Jan. 16, 1863.

> *By order of*
> *Robert E. Lee,*
> *Lieutenant General Commanding*

Jack never forgot the dismal night and the march which followed it. They tied a handkerchief over his head and led him a little apart to a wall which bounded one side of the camp. Never had life seemed so sweet.

General Lee in his tent thought long and seriously upon the matter.

"He is so awfully young and of good family too; but camp discipline must be enforced. Still it was not much of an offense for such a punishment. The lad was over tired and wounded. By George, he shall go free if I risk my reputation. Sergeant, order private John Sanderson to be brought before me."

"Very well, sir," and saluting, the orderly left the tent.

Jack was brought in, supported by two soldiers, for a reaction had set in after his narrow escape from death.

"Sir," said General Lee sternly, "on account of your extreme youth you will get off with a reprimand but see that it never happens again, for, if it should, I shall not be so lenient."

"General," answered Jack drawing himself up to his full height, "the Confederate States of America shall never have cause to regret that I was not shot;" and Jack was led away, still trembling, but happy in the knowledge of a new found life.

Six weeks after with Lee's army near Chancellorsville. The success of Fredericksburg had made possible this advance of the Confederate arms. The firing had just commenced when a courier rode up to General Jackson.

"Colonel Barrows says, sir, that the enemy have possession of a small frame house on the outskirts of the woods and it overlooks our earthworks. Has he your permission to take it by assault?"

"My compliments to Colonel Barrows and say that I cannot spare more than twenty men but that he is welcome to charge with that number," answered the General.

"Yes, sir," and the orderly, setting spurs to his horse, rode away.

Five minutes later a column of men from the 3rd Virginia burst out from the woods and ran toward the house. A galling fire broke out from the Federal lines and many a brave man fell, among whom was their leader, a young lieutenant. Jack Sanderson sprang to the front and waving his gun encouraged the men onward. Half way between the Confederate lines and the house was a small mound, and behind this the men threw themselves to get a minute's respite.

A minute later a figure sprang up and ran toward the house, and before the Union troops saw him he was halfway across the bullet swept clearing. Then the federal fire was directed at him. He staggered for a moment and placed his hand to his forehead. On he ran and reaching the house, he quickly opened the door and went inside. A minute later a pillar of flame shot out of the windows of the house and almost immediately afterwards the Federal occupants were in full flight. A long cheer rolled along the Confederate lines and then the word was given to charge and they charged sweeping all before them. That night the searchers wended their way to the half burned house. There on the floor, beside the mattress he had set on fire, lay the body of him who had once been John Sanderson, private, 3rd Virginia. He had paid his debt.

Dead Confederate soldier in the trenches
of Fort Mahone in Virginia, 1865.

THE GREAT DRAFT RIOTS

SUSAN HAYES

By late 1863, support for the war was dwindling in the North. Lincoln and Congress instituted a draft to increase manpower for the army. However, wealthy individuals were able to escape service by paying a fee. New York, with its high immigrant population too poor to pay, became the site of a large riot.

At 7:00 a.m. on a typical day in New York City in the 1860s, the docks lining the city's waterfront were teeming with workers. The Civil War (1861–1865) was raging, and every day dozens of ships entered the harbor to load and unload supplies. But on the hot, steamy morning of Monday, July 13, 1863, the docks were nearly empty. Suddenly, around 7:15 a.m., a mob of angry men brandishing weapons and hand-lettered signs that said "NO DRAFT" surged onto the waterfront. They grabbed the few workers who had shown up for work and closed down the docks. The great New York City draft riots had begun—the first major urban riot in American history and the deadliest until the 1900s.

The riots broke out in the midst of the gravest crisis in the young nation's history. And it occurred at a low point in the North's fortunes. Its all-volunteer Union Army was losing the war to the Southern Confederacy, suffering defeat after defeat.

With morale low, the North found recruiting difficult, even after offering cash bonuses, or bounties, of as much as $1,000. In 1862, the Confederacy had dealt with the same problem by instituting a draft—the first government-imposed draft in U.S. history.

Now, with the Union at stake, President Abraham Lincoln begged Congress to do the same in the North. It did, on March 3, 1863. Under

The *Tribune*, a pro-draft newspaper, was a target for rioting New Yorkers.

the draft, all white men age 20 to 45 were in the draft pool. But there was a catch. Any man who paid $300 cash to the government was excused. For the rich, this was no problem. But for the poor, especially the tens of thousands of Irish and other immigrants living in cities like New York, $300 was a year's wages. "This is a rich man's [draft], made for him who can raise $300 and against him who cannot raise that sum," railed U.S. Representative Thaddeus Stevens of Pennsylvania.

The draft went into effect in New York City on July 11. By the next day, the city's Irish slums—where most draftees came from—were seething. On the morning of July 13, thousands marched to Central Park, where they listened to incendiary speeches urging them to oppose the draft. From there, it was on to the draft office and the streets.

Here, in the words of contemporary observers, and the rioters themselves, is what happened next.

A PROTEST TURNS VIOLENT What began as an organized protest march quickly turned violent when the angry protesters set fire to the draft office. One New York City woman kept a daily diary of the riots. Here, she describes the events of the first day.

> "All day yesterday there were dreadful scenes enacted in the city. The police were successfully opposed; many were killed, many houses were gutted and burned; Negroes were hung in the streets! All last night the firebells rang, but at last the rain came down in torrents and scattered the crowds, giving the city authorities time to get organized."
>
> —*Maria L. Daly*
>
> *July 14, 1863*

Many immigrants were fearful that freed slaves would move north and take away their jobs if the North won the war. Thus, the rioters harbored a particular hatred toward blacks. On the afternoon of the first day of the riots, the rioters looted and then set fire to the city's black orphanage. There were 230 children ages 4 to 12 in the home at the time.

> "About four hundred [people] entered the house and proceeded to pitch out beds, chairs, tables, and every species of furniture, which were eagerly seized by the crowd below, and carried off. When all was taken, the house was then set on fire.
>
> "While the rioters were clamoring for admittance at the front door, the Matron and Superintendent were quietly and rapidly conducting the children out the backyard, down to the police station."
>
> —*Report of the Committee of Merchants*
> *for the Relief of Colored People*
> *Suffering from the Late Riots in the*
> *City of New York*
>
> *July 20,1863*

A RIOTER SPEAKS OUT As the violence spread, one rioter took the time to compose and send a letter to *The New York Times*, defending his actions and those of his comrades. It was published two days later.

Monday Night, Uptown

To the Editor:

You will no doubt be hard on us rioters tomorrow morning, but that 300-dollar law has made us nobodies, vagabonds and cast-outs of society, for whom nobody cares when we must go to war and be shot down. We are the poor rabble, and the rich rabble is our enemy by this law. Although we've got hard fists, and are dirty without, we have soft hearts and have clean consciences within, and that's the reason we love our wives and children more than the rich, because we've not got much besides them; and we will not go and leave them at home for to starve.

A Poor Man, But a Man for All That[1]

Wednesday, July 15, 1863

On the riots' second day, New York Governor Horatio Seymour addressed a huge crowd in front of City Hall. Many in the crowd waved signs reading "No Draft" and "The Poor Man's Blood for the Rich Man's Money." Although Seymour later claimed he was simply trying to stop the violence, many city leaders condemned him for being too soft on the rioters. This speech later cost Seymour his political career.

"I am your friend. I implore you to take care that no man's property or person is injured. I rely on you, and if you refrain from further riotous acts, I will see to it that your rights shall be protected. The question of the legality of the Conscription Act will go before the Courts. If the Act be declared legal, I pledge myself, the State, and the city authorities to see that there should be no inequality between the rich and the poor."

—Governor Horatio Seymour

July 14, 1863

1 **A Poor Man, But a Man for All That:** the author of the letter sent it anonymously and signed it with an allusion to a poem by 18th century poet Robert Burns—"A man's a man for a' that." The letter writer's intent was to point out that the poor might not have the wealth to escape the draft, but they were still people who deserved respect.

From the start, the influential newspaper *The New York Times* had condemned the rioters. *The Times* published this editorial defending the fairness of the draft.

> "Conscription is a necessity; the conscription is a law; the conscription is just. It is the justest mode of raising an army—just to the people of every class and condition, poor and rich, black and white. No class of citizens is exempt from its operation—even poor clergymen, if drafted, being compelled to shoulder their musket."
>
> —*The New York Times*
>
> *July 15, 1863*

THE DRAFT RIOTS' LEGACY By July 16, hundreds of people were dead and millions of dollars' worth of property was destroyed. With the draft office in ruins and the Governor's promise to look into the draftees' grievances, the riots petered out. Meanwhile, Union soldiers, fresh from their victory at Gettysburg, arrived in the city to restore order. The insurrection was over.

A few weeks later, President Lincoln turned down Governor Seymour's request to reconsider the draft.

> "I can not consent to suspend the draft in New York, as you request, because, among other reasons, time is too important. We are contending with an enemy who drives every able-bodied man he can reach into its ranks. It produces an army with a rapidity not to be matched on our side, if we first waste time to re-experiment with the volunteer system."
>
> —*President Abraham Lincoln*
>
> *August 7, 1863*

The draft resumed in New York City without incident on August 19, 1863. Ten thousand Union soldiers patrolled the city streets. In the end, only 7 percent of those drafted in the North ever wound up serving in the Union Army. But the draft riots left a long-standing legacy. As America and its cities grew after the Civil War, the class, racial, and immigrant anger that fueled the draft riots would reappear again, in an even more violent fashion.

GETTYSBURG

GARY PAULSEN

It was in many respects exactly the same and yet completely different.
He had been in more skirmishes and he had killed more men. He had
men die next to him. But he had not been in another major battle.

Now he was at Gettysburg, Pennsylvania, on top of a gradually sloping
hill, looking down at what seemed to be the entire Southern army assembling to attack.

THE BATTLE OF GETTYSBURG
painted 1863 James Walker

What was the same was the meadow. There was always a forest and always a meadow. In this case the forest where the Rebels were assembling was over a mile away and well below the Union army. In between was a large meadow a mile or more wide. The Rebels would have to leave the trees and walk, under constant fire from artillery, across the meadow and up the incline to the fences and rock walls where the Union soldiers waited.

What was different about this battle was that Charley was above the Rebs, in a sheltered position, with all the guns in the world behind him.

It was a warm day and he sipped some water from his canteen and checked his rifle. He had taken a new one from a dead man after his own had been destroyed. This rifle had a tendency to foul its nipple, so he carried a small needle stuck in his shirt to clean the hole out if it plugged. He did so now and put a fresh cap on the nipple, then tightened his shoelaces in case he had to run. That was always in his mind—either run at them or run away. He did not want to stumble.

He peeked through the rock wall again and saw the Confederate artillery wheeling their cannon into place. The Rebs would try to prepare the hill with artillery before their charge, and as Charley looked the first batteries began firing. Soon they were all hammering away. It was the

worst barrage Charley had undergone. Shells burst overhead and killed men and horses and destroyed some Union artillery and rear positions. But it could have been far worse. The line of Union troops waiting to take the Confederate attack were at the brow of the hill, which dropped away to their rear as well. The Rebel artillery was massed and firing heavily, but rounds aimed at the top of the hill that went even slightly high just passed over and exploded down the back side.

Casualties were not as heavy as all the noise and smoke indicated. When shooting tapered off and the Rebels started moving their massed troops across the meadow and up the hill, the Union artillery wheeled into position and tore into them with exploding rounds: chain and grapeshot. The Confederates had to march through a storm of fire and Charley lay and watched them and nearly felt sorry for them.

They were so brave, he thought—or foolish. They kept coming, even when thousands of them were down and dying. The cannon ripped them to pieces, wiping them out before they were even within rifle range, slaughtering them like sheep as they marched in even rows. Sometimes whole rows were dropped where they stood, so the dead lay in orderly lines. And still they came on.

At first it all seemed so distant, as if it was a staged tableau. Men marched, then they spun and fell, exploding red bursts into the air.

But as they came closer and Charley could see what the artillery was doing to them—tearing, gutting, blowing apart—he could not believe that anyone would continue, *could* continue against the fire.

Yet they came on and on, close enough now so those not hit could return fire, and Charley could hear their bullets hitting the rocks in front of him and he thought, so this is what it's like to be safe, to fight from a good position.

"All right—up, men." The sergeants roused them. "Ready to fire! Shoot low, shoot low—take their legs out. Present, aim, fire!"

Charley raised, aimed and fired, all in less than two seconds. He did not know if he hit, did not care. He reloaded behind the wall, rose, aimed, fired, and thought, this is the way it should be done. The bullets over his head sounded like a storm but they were all high, and he kept reloading and firing as the remaining Rebs screamed and started to run at the wall.

"Up, men! Bayonets! Take them."

Charley did not think any of the Rebels would reach the line but they came on. Torn and bleeding and many in rags, they yelled and came with bayonets, and for a moment it seemed they would carry it, win the hill, win the battle against impossible odds.

But a colonel saw the danger and ordered the only unit still in relative shelter—the First Minnesota Volunteers—to make a counter-charge.

They rose and went as one man, Charley among them. Screaming their own yells, they tore down the hill at the Rebel unit storming up the hill, and the two bodies of men collided in a smash of steel and powder, standing toe-to-toe, hacking and shooting at each other, neither giving, climbing over the bodies of friends to hit enemies, Charley in the middle jabbing and screaming until he was hit, and hit again, spun and knocked down, and he saw the red veil come down over his eyes and knew that at last he was right, at last he was done, at last he was dead.

Field Notes

Battle: Gettysburg

Location: Gettysburg, Pennsylvania

Date: July 1-3, 1863

Commanding Officers:

    Confederate Robert E. Lee

    Union George Gordon Meade

Behind the lines: Neither general wanted to fight on hilly terrain. Confederates on a mission into Gettysburg for shoes were caught by a Union patrol. Lee was unaware the Union army was so close because his "eyes and ears"— J.E.B. Stuart and the Confederate cavalry—were raiding near Washington, D.C. The Confederate defeats here and at Vicksburg were the turning point of the war.

Winner: Union

THE GETTYSBURG ADDRESS

ABRAHAM LINCOLN

Lincoln gave this address at the dedication of the battlefield at
Gettysburg, Pennsylvania, on November 19, 1863. He used this speech
to renew support for the war, which many thought was lasting far
too long, and at too great a price.

Four score and seven years ago our fathers brought forth on this continent, a new nation, conceived in Liberty, and dedicated to the proposition that all men are created equal.

Now we are engaged in a great civil war, testing whether that nation, or any nation so conceived and so dedicated, can long endure. We are met on a great battlefield of that war. We have come to dedicate a portion of that field, as a final resting place for those who here gave their lives that this nation might live. It is altogether fitting and proper that we should do this.

But, in a larger sense, we can not dedicate—we can not consecrate—we can not hallow—this ground. The brave men, living and dead, who struggled here, have consecrated it, far above our poor power to add or detract. The world will little note, nor long remember what we say here, but it can never forget what they did here. It is for us the living, rather, to be dedicated here to the unfinished work which they who fought here have thus far so nobly advanced. It is rather for us to be here dedicated to the great task remaining before us—that from these honored dead we take increased devotion to that cause for which they gave the last full measure of devotion—that we here highly resolve that these dead shall not have died in vain—that this nation, under God, shall have a new birth of freedom—and that government of the people, by the people, for the people, shall not perish from the earth.

WILLIAM CLARKE QUANTRILL

(1837-1865)

The Missouri-Kansas border had been a hotbed of civil unrest since the passage of the Kansas-Nebraska Act in 1854. Slavery and anti-slavery forces regularly raided on both sides of the border, killing anyone thought to be a supporter of the opposing side. William Quantrill was one of the more brutal raiders. He was a military strategist with a charismatic personality. The raid on Lawrence, Kansas, was retribution for the deaths of several of the raiders' mothers, sisters, and wives. The women were kept under U.S. Army guard in a dilapidated building in Kansas City which collapsed. Quantrill and his raiders held the Union army responsible and decided to retaliate by killing Union supporters in Lawrence.

Leader of perhaps the most savage fighting unit in the Civil War, William Quantrill developed a style of guerrilla warfare that terrorized civilians and soldiers alike.

Quantrill was born in 1837 in Ohio, but little is known of his early life. It appears that after being a schoolteacher for several years, he traveled to Utah in 1858 with an army wagon train and there made his living as a gambler, using the alias of Charles Hart. After a year, he moved to Lawrence, Kansas, where he was again a schoolteacher from 1859 to 1860. But his past and predisposition soon caught up with him and, wanted for murder and horse theft, Quantrill fled to Missouri in late 1860.

Quantrill entered the Civil War on the Confederate side with enthusiasm. By late 1861, he was the leader of Quantrill's Raiders, a small force of no more than a dozen men who harassed Union soldiers and sympathizers along the Kansas-Missouri border and often clashed with Jayhawkers, the pro-Union guerrilla bands that reversed Quantrill's tactics by staging raids from Kansas into Missouri. Union forces soon declared him an outlaw, and the Confederacy officially made him a captain. To his supporters in Missouri, he was a dashing, free-spirited hero.

The climax of Quantrill's guerrilla career came on August 21, 1863, when he led a force of 450 raiders into Lawrence, Kansas, a stronghold of pro-Union support and the home of Senator James H. Lane, whose leading

The raid on Lawrence, Kansas, 1863.

William Clarke Quantrill

role in the struggle for free-soil[1] in Kansas had made him a public enemy to pro-slavery forces in Missouri. Lane managed to escape, racing through a cornfield in his nightshirt, but Quantrill and his men killed 183 men and boys, dragging some from their homes to murder them in front of their families, and set the torch to much of the city.

The Lawrence Massacre led to swift retribution, as Union troops forced the residents of four Missouri border counties onto the open prairie while Jayhawkers looted and burned everything they left behind. Quantrill and his raiders took part in the Confederate retaliation for this atrocity, but when Union forces drove the Confederates back, Quantrill fled to Texas. His guerrilla band broke up into several smaller units, including one headed by his vicious lieutenant, "Bloody Bill" Anderson, known for wearing a necklace of Yankee scalps into battle. Quantrill himself was eventually killed on a raid into Kentucky in 1865.

Even after his death, Quantrill and his followers remained almost folk heroes to their supporters in Missouri, and something of this celebrity later rubbed off on several ex-Raiders—the James brothers, Frank and Jesse, and the Younger brothers, Cole and Jim—who went on in the late 1860s to apply Quantrill's hit-and-run tactics to bank and train robbery, building on his legacy of bloodshed a mythology of the Western outlaw that remains fixed in the popular imagination.

1 **free-soil:** a political party that worked to keep slavery out of new states

RESPONDING TO CLUSTER TWO

A TURNING POINT?

Thinking Skill COMPARING AND CONTRASTING

1. Do you think the rioters in "The Great Draft Riots" were justified in their actions against the draft? Use details from the selection to support your answer.

2. Lincoln's "Gettysburg Address" is considered one of the greatest speeches ever delivered. Besides memorializing the dead of the battle at Gettysburg, he also hoped to inspire the North to continue the war against the South. Find three phrases in the speech that might persuade the North to continue fighting.

3. **Compare and contrast** Jack Sanderson in "A Debt of Honor" and Charley Goddard in "Gettysburg." Which character seems more realistic? Be prepared to support your choice.

4. Imagine you are a newspaper editor in 1863 preparing to write an editorial on the current state of the war. **Compare and contrast** both sides in the war and decide which you think stands the best chance of winning the war. In a short outline, state which side you believe will win and three reasons why.

Writing Activity: A Letter Home

Imagine you are one of the soldiers in Cluster One or Cluster Two writing a letter home. **Contrast** the feelings you had at the beginning of the war with your feelings about the progress of the war now—1863. You will have to make up the name of the person you are writing to, the place you are writing from, and the date.

Writing a Personal Letter

• include the date, place you are writing from, and address of the person you are writing to

• a personal letter can be informal; but remember, people of the Civil War period would not be familiar with today's slang terms

• the content of your letter should include details that the receiver of the letter will find interesting

CLUSTER THREE

1864-1865: What Were the Costs of the War?

Thinking Skill SUMMARIZING

The ruins of Richmond, Virginia, 1865.

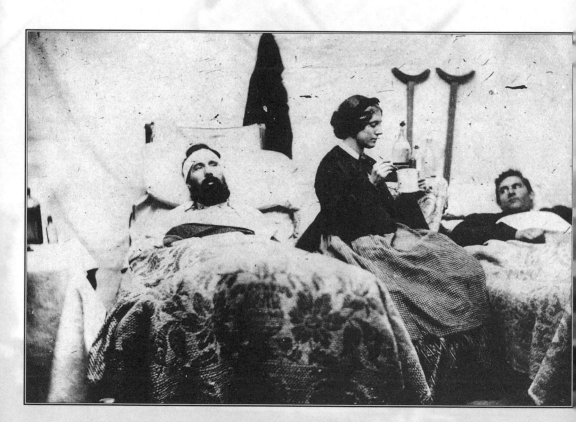

A nurse tends to patients at a hospital in Nashville, Tennessee.

THE BLUE AND THE GRAY
A HOSPITAL SKETCH

LOUISA MAY ALCOTT

D on't bring him in here; every corner is full—and I'm glad of it," added the nurse under her breath, eyeing with strong disfavor the gaunt figure lying on the stretcher in the doorway.

"Where *shall* we put him, then? They won't have him in either of the other wards on this floor. He's ordered up here, and here he must stay if he's put in the hall—poor devil!" said the foremost bearer, looking around the crowded room in despair.

The nurse's eye followed his, and both saw a thin hand beckoning from the end of the long ward.

"It's Murry; I'll see what he wants;" and Miss Mercy went to him with her quick, noiseless step, and the smile her grave face always wore for him.

"There's room here, if you turn my bed 'round, you see. Don't let them leave him in the hall," said Murry, lifting his great eyes to hers. Brilliant with the fever burning his strength away, and pathetic with the silent protest of life against death.

"It's like you to think of it; but he's a rebel," began Miss Mercy.

"So much more reason to take him in. I don't mind having him here; but it will distress me dreadfully to know that any poor soul was turned away, from the comfort of this ward especially."

The look he gave her made the words an eloquent compliment, and his pity for a fallen enemy reproached her for her own lack of it. Her face softened as she nodded, and glanced about the recess.

"You will have the light in your eyes, and only the little table between you and a very disagreeable neighbor," she said.

"I can shut my eyes if the light troubles them; I've nothing else to do now," he answered, with a faint laugh. "I was too comfortable before; I'd more than my share of luxuries; so bring him along, and it will be all right."

The order was given, and, after a brief bustle, the two narrow beds stood side by side in the recess under the organ-loft—for the hospital had been a church. Left alone for a moment, the two men eyed each other silently. Murry saw a tall, sallow man, with fierce black eyes, wild hair and beard, and thin-lipped, cruel mouth. A ragged gray uniform was visible under the blanket thrown over him; and in strange contrast to the squalor of his dress, and the neglect of his person, was the diamond ring that shone on his unwounded hand. The right arm was bound up, the right leg amputated at the knee; and though the man's face was white and haggard with suffering, not a sound escaped him as he lay with his bold eyes fixed defiantly upon his neighbor.

John Clay, the new-comer, saw opposite him a small, wasted figure, and a plain face; yet both face and figure were singularly attractive, for suffering seemed to have refined away all the grosser elements, and left the spiritual very visible through that frail tenement[1] of flesh. Pale-brown hair streaked the hollow temples and white forehead. A deep color burned in the thin cheeks still tanned by the wind and weather of a long campaign. The mouth was grave and sweet, and in the gray eyes lay an infinite patience touched with melancholy. He wore a dressing-gown, but across his feet lay a faded coat of army-blue. As the other watched him, he saw a shadow pass across his tranquil face, and for a moment he laid his wasted hand over the eyes that had been so full of pity. Then he gently pushed a mug of fresh water, and the last of a bunch of grapes, toward the exhausted rebel, saying, in a cordial tone,

"You look faint and thirsty; have 'em."

Clay's lips were parched, and his hand went involuntarily toward the cup; but he caught it back, and leaning forward, asked in a shrill whisper,

"Where are you hurt?"

"A shot in the side," answered Murry, visibly surprised at the man's manner.

"What battle?"

---

1 **frail tenement:** thin, weak body

"The Wilderness."

"Is it bad?"

"I'm dying of wound-fever; there's no hope, they say."

That reply, so simple, so serenely given, would have touched almost any hearer; but Clay smiled grimly, and lay down as if satisfied, with his one hand clenched, and an exulting glitter in his eyes, muttering to himself.

"The loss of my leg comes easier after hearing that."

Murry saw his lips move, but caught no sound, and asked with friendly solicitude,

"Do you want any thing, neighbor?"

"Yes—to be let alone," was the curt reply, with a savage frown.

"That's easily done. I shan't trouble you very long, any way;" and, with a sigh, Murry turned his face away, and lay silent till the surgeon came up on his morning round.

"Oh, you're here, are you? It's like Mercy Carrol to take you in," said Dr. Fitz Hugh as he surveyed the rebel with a slight frown; for, in spite of his benevolence and skill, he was a stanch loyalist, and hated the South as he did sin.

"Don't praise me; he never would have been here but for Murry," answered Miss Mercy, as she approached with her dressing-tray in her hand.

"Bless the lad! he'll give up his bed next, and feel offended if he's thanked for it. How are you, my good fellow?" and the doctor turned to press the hot hand with a friendly face.

"Much easier and stronger, thank you, doctor," was the cheerful answer.

"Less fever, pulse better, breath free—good symptoms. Keep on so for twenty-four hours, and by my soul, I believe you'll have a chance for your life, Murry," cried the doctor, as his experienced eye took note of a hopeful change.

"In spite of the opinion of three good surgeons to the contrary?" asked Murry, with a wistful smile.

"Hang every body's opinions! We are but mortal men, and the best of us make mistakes in spite of science and experience. There's Parker; we all gave him up, and the rascal is larking 'round Washington as well as ever to-day. While there's life, there's hope; so cheer up, my lad, and do your best for the little girl at home."

"Do you really think I may hope?" cried Murry, white with the joy of this unexpected reprieve.

"Hope is a capital medicine, and I prescribe it for a day at least. Don't build on this change too much, but if you are as well to-morrow as this morning, I give you my word I think you'll pull through."

Murry laid his hands over his face with a broken "Thank God for that!" and the doctor turned away with a sonorous "Hem!" and an air of intense satisfaction.

During this conversation Miss Mercy had been watching the rebel, who looked and listened to the others so intently that he forgot her presence. She saw an expression of rage and disappointment gather in his face as the doctor spoke; and when Murry accepted the hope held out to him, Clay set his teeth with an evil look, that would have boded ill for his neighbor had he not been helpless.

"Ungrateful traitor! I'll watch him, for he'll do mischief if he can," she thought, and reluctantly began to unbind his arm for the doctor's inspection.

"Only a flesh-wound—no bones broken—a good syringing, rubber cushion, plenty of water, and it will soon heal. You'll attend to that Miss Mercy; this stump is more in my line;" and Dr. Fitz Hugh turned to the leg, leaving the arm to the nurse's skillful care.

"Evidently amputated in a hurry, and neglected since. If you're not careful, young man, you'll change places with your neighbor here."

"Damn him!" muttered Clay in his beard, with an emphasis which caused the doctor to glance at his vengeful face.

"Don't be a brute, if you can help it. But for him, you'd have fared ill," began the doctor.

"But for him, I never should have been here," muttered the man in French, with a furtive glance about the room.

"You owe this to him?" asked the doctor, touching the wound, and speaking in the same tongue.

"Yes; but he paid for it—at least, I thought he had."

"By the Lord! if you are the sneaking rascal that shot him as he lay wounded in the ambulance, I shall be tempted to leave you to your fate!" cried the doctor, with a wrathful flash in his keen eyes.

"Do it, then, for it was I," answered the man defiantly; adding as if anxious to explain, "We had a tussle, and each got hurt in the thick of the skirmish. He was put in the ambulance afterward, and I was left to live or die, as luck would have it. I was hurt the worst; they should have taken me too; it made me mad to see him chosen, and I fired my last shot as he drove away. I didn't know whether I hit him or not; but when they told me I must lose my leg, I hoped I had, and now I am satisfied."

He spoke rapidly, with clenched hand and fiery eyes, and the two listeners watched him with a sort of fascination as he hissed out the last words, glancing at the occupant of the next bed. Murry evidently did not understand French; he lay with averted face, closed eyes, and a hopeful smile still on his lips, quite unconscious of the meaning of the fierce words uttered close beside him. Dr. Fitz Hugh had laid down his instrument and knit his black brows irefully while he listened. But as the man paused, the doctor looked at Miss Mercy, who was quietly going on with her work, though there was an expression about her handsome mouth that made her womanly face look almost grim. Taking up his tools, the doctor followed her example, saying slowly,

"If I didn't believe Murry was mending, I'd turn you over to Roberts, whom the patients dread as they do the devil. I must do my duty, and you may thank Murry for it."

"Does he know you are the man who shot him?" asked Mercy, still in French.

"No; I shouldn't stay here long if he did," answered Clay, with a short laugh.

"Don't tell him, then—at least, till after you are moved," she said, in a tone of command.

"Where am I going?" demanded the man.

"Anywhere out of my ward," was the brief answer, with a look that made the black eyes waver and fall.

In the silence nurse and doctor did their work, and passed on. In silence Murry lay hour after hour, and silently did Clay watch and wait, till, utterly exhausted by the suffering he was too proud to confess, he sank into a stupor, oblivious alike of hatred, defeat, and pain. Finding him in this pitiable condition, Mercy relented, and woman-like, forgot her contempt in pity. He was not moved, but tended carefully all that day and night; and when he woke from a heavy sleep, the morning sun shone again on two pale faces in the beds, and flashed on the buttons of two army-coats hanging side by side on the recess wall, on loyalist and rebel, on the blue and the gray.

Dr. Fitz Hugh stood beside Murry's cot, saying cheerily, "You are doing well, my lad—better than I hoped. Keep calm and cool, and, if all goes right, we'll have little Mary here to pet you in a week."

"Who's Mary?" whispered the rebel to the attendant who was washing his face.

"His sweetheart; he left her for the war, and she's waitin' for him back —poor soul!" answered the man, with a somewhat vicious scrub across the sallow cheek he was wiping.

"So he'll get well, and go home and marry the girl he left behind him, will he?" sneered Clay, fingering a little case that hung about his neck, and was now visible as his rough valet unbuttoned his collar.

"What's that—your sweetheart's picter?" asked Ben, the attendant, eyeing the gold chain anxiously.

"I've got none," was the gruff answer.

"So much the wus for you, then. Small chance of gettin' one here; our girls won't look at you, and you a'n't likely to see any of your own sort for a long spell, I reckon," added Ben, rasping away at the rebel's long-neglected hair.

Clay lay looking at Mercy Carrol as she went to and fro among the men, leaving a smile behind her, and carrying comfort wherever she turned,—a right womanly woman, lovely and lovable, strong yet tender, patient yet decided, skillful, kind, and tireless in the discharge of duties that would have daunted most women. It was in vain she wore the plain gray gown and long apron, for neither could hide the grace of her figure. It was in vain she brushed her luxuriant hair back into a net, for the wavy locks would fall on her forehead, and stray curls would creep out or glisten like gold under the meshes meant to conceal them. Busy days and watchful nights had not faded the beautiful bloom on her cheeks, or dimmed the brightness of her hazel eyes. Always ready, fresh, and fair, Mercy Carrol was regarded as the good angel of the hospital, and not a man in it, sick or well, but was a loyal friend to her. None dared to be a lover, for her little romance was known; and, though still a maid, she was a widow in their eyes, for she had sent her lover to his death, and over the brave man's grave had said, "Well done."

Ben watched Clay as his eye followed the one female figure there, and observing that he clutched the case still tighter, asked again,

"What is that—a charm?"

"Yes—against pain, captivity, and shame."

"Strikes me it a'n't kep' you from any one of 'em," said Ben, with a laugh.

"I haven't tried it yet."

"How does it work?" Ben asked more respectfully, being impressed by something in the rebel's manner.

"You will see when I use it. Now let me alone;" and Clay turned impatiently away.

"You've got p'ison, or some deviltry, in that thing. If you don't let me look, I swear I'll have it took away from you"; and Ben put his big hand on the slender chain with a resolute air.

Clay smiled a scornful smile, and offered the trinket, saying coolly,

"I only fooled you. Look as much as you like; you'll find nothing dangerous."

Ben opened the pocket, saw a curl of gray hair, and nothing more.

"Is that your mother's?"

"Yes; my dead mother's."

It was strange to see the instantaneous change that passed over the two men as each uttered that dearest word in all tongues. Rough Ben gently reclosed and returned the case, saying kindly,

"Keep it; I wouldn't rob you on't for no money."

Clay thrust it jealously into his breast, and the first trace of emotion he had shown softened his dark face, as he answered, with a grateful tremor in his voice,

"Thank you. I wouldn't lose it for the world."

"May I say good morning, neighbor?" asked a feeble voice, as Murry turned a very wan but cheerful face toward him, when Ben moved on with his basin and towel.

"If you like," returned Clay, looking at him with those quick, suspicious eyes of his.

"Well, I do like, so I say it, and hope you are better," returned the cordial voice.

"Are you?"

"Yes, thank God!"

"Is it sure?"

"Nothing is sure, in a case like mine, till I'm on my legs again; but I'm certainly better. I don't expect *you* to be glad, but I hope you don't regret it very much."

"I don't." The smile that accompanied the words surprised Murry as much as the reply, for both seemed honest, and his kind heart warmed toward his suffering enemy.

"I hope you'll be exchanged as soon as you are able. Till then, you can go to one of the other hospitals where there are many reb—I would say, Southerners. If you'd like, I'll speak to Dr. Fitz Hugh, and he'll see you moved," said Murry, in his friendly way.

"I'd rather stay here, thank you." Clay smiled again as he spoke in the mild tone that surprised Murry as much as it pleased him.

"You like to be in my corner, then?" he said, with a boyish laugh.

"Very much—for a while."

"I shall suffer more by and by, if I go on; but I'll risk it," answered Clay, fixing his feverish eyes on Murry's placid face.

"You expect to have a hard time with your leg?" said Murry, compassionately.

"With my soul."

It was an odd answer, and given with such an odd expression, as Clay turned his face away, that Murry said no more, fancying his brain a little touched by the fever evidently coming on.

They spoke but seldom to each other that day, for Clay lay apparently asleep, with a flushed cheek and restless head, and Murry tranquilly dreamed waking dreams of home and little Mary. That night, after all was still, Miss Mercy went up into the organ-loft to get fresh rollers for the morrow—the boxes of old linen, and such matters, being kept there. As she stood looking down on the thirty pale sleepers, she remembered that she had not played a hymn on the little organ for Murry, as she had promised that day. Stealing softly to the front, she peeped over the gallery, to see if he was asleep; if not, she would keep her word, for he was her favorite.

A screen had been drawn before the recess where the two beds stood, shutting their occupants from the sight of the other men. Murry lay sleeping, but Clay was awake, and a quick thrill tingled along the young woman's nerves as she saw his face. Leaning on one arm, he peered about the place with an eager, watchful air, and glanced up at the dark gallery, but did not see the startled face behind the central pillar. Pausing an instant, he shook his one clenched hand at the unconscious sleeper, and then drew out the locket cautiously. Two white mugs just alike stood on the little table between the beds, water in each. With another furtive glance about him, Clay suddenly stretched out his long arm, and dropped something from the locket into Murry's cup. An instant he remained motionless, with a sinister smile on his face; then, as Ben's step sounded beyond the screen, he threw his arm over his face, and lay, breathing heavily, as if asleep.

Mercy's first impulse was to cry out; her next, to fly down and seize the cup. No time was to be lost, for Murry might wake and drink at any moment. What was in the cup? Poison, doubtless; that was the charm

Clay carried to free himself from "pain, captivity, and shame," when all other hopes of escape vanished. This hidden helper he gave up to destroy his enemy, who was to outlive his shot, it seemed. Like a shadow, Mercy glided down, forming her plan as she went. A dozen mugs stood about the room, all alike in size and color; catching up one, she partly filled it, and, concealing it under the clean sheet hanging on her arm, went toward the recess, saying audibly,

"I want some fresh water, Ben."

Thus warned of her approach,

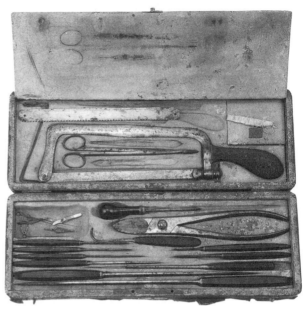

Surgeon's instrument kit

Clay lay with carefully-averted face as she came in, and never stirred as she bent over him, while she dexterously changed Murry's mug for the one she carried. Hiding the poisoned cup, she went away, saying aloud,

"Never mind the water, now, Ben. Murry is asleep, and so is Clay; they'll not need it yet."

Straight to Dr. Fitz Hugh's room she went, and gave the cup into his keeping, with the story of what she had seen. A man was dying, and there was not time to test the water then; but putting it carefully away, he promised to set her fears at rest in the morning. To quiet her impatience, Mercy went back to watch over Murry till day dawned. As she sat down, she caught the glimmer of a satisfied smile on Clay's lips, and looking into the cup she had left, she saw that it was empty.

"He is satisfied, for he thinks his horrible revenge is secure. Sleep in peace, my poor boy! you are safe while I am here."

As she thought this, she put her hand on the broad, pale forehead of the sleeper with a motherly caress, but started to feel how damp and cold it was. Looking nearer, she saw that a change had passed over Murry, for dark shadows showed about his sunken eyes, his once quiet breath was faint and fitful now, his hand deathly cold, and a chilly dampness had gathered on his face. She looked at her watch; it was past twelve, and her heart sunk within her, for she had so often seen that solemn change come over men's faces then, that the hour was doubly weird and woeful to her. Sending a message to Dr. Fitz Hugh, she waited anxiously, trying to believe that she deceived herself.

The doctor came at once, and a single look convinced him that he had left one death-bed for another.

"As I feared," he said; "that sudden rally was but a last effort of nature. There was just once chance for him, and he has missed it. Poor lad! I can do nothing; he'll sink rapidly, and go without pain."

"Can *I* do nothing?" asked Mercy, with dim eyes, as she held the cold hand close in both her own with tender pressure.

"Give him stimulants as long as he can swallow, and, if he's conscious, take any messages he may have. Poor Hall is dying hard, and I can help him; I'll come again in an hour and say good-by."

The kind doctor choked, touched the pale sleeper with a gentle caress, and went away to help Hall die.

Murry slept on for an hour, then woke, and knew without words that his brief hope was gone. He looked up wistfully, and whispered, as Mercy tried to smile with trembling lips that refused to tell the heavy truth.

"I know, I feel it; don't grieve yourself by trying to tell me, dear friend. It's best so; I can bear it, but I did want to live."

"Have you any word for Mary, dear?" asked Mercy, for he seemed but a boy to her since she had nursed him.

One look of sharp anguish and dark despair passed over his face, as he wrung his thin hands and shut his eyes, finding death terrible. It passed in a moment, and his pallid countenance grew beautiful with the pathetic patience of one who submits without complaint to the inevitable.

"Tell her I was ready, and the only bitterness was leaving her. I shall remember, and wait until she comes. My little Mary! oh, be kind to her, for my sake, when you tell her this."

"I will, Murry, as Gods hears me. I will be a sister to her while I live."

As Mercy spoke with fervent voice, he laid the hand that had ministered to him so faithfully against his cheek, and lay silent, as if content.

"What else? let me do something more. Is there no other friend to be comforted?"

"No; she is all I have in the world. I hoped to make her so happy, to be so much to her, for she's a lonely little thing; but God says 'No,' and I submit."

A long pause, as he lay breathing heavily, with eyes that were dimming fast fixed on the gentle face beside him.

"Give Ben my clothes; send Mary a bit of my hair, and—may I give you this? It's a poor thing, but all I have to leave you, best and kindest of women."

He tried to draw off a slender ring, but the strength had gone out of his wasted fingers, and she helped him, thanking him with the first tears he had seen her shed. He seemed satisfied, but suddenly turned his eyes on Clay, who lay as if asleep. A sigh broke from Murry, and Mercy caught the words.

"How could he do it, and I so helpless!"

"Do you know him?" she whispered, eagerly, as she remembered Clay's own words.

"I knew he was the man who shot me, when he came. I forgive him; but I wish he had spared me, for Mary's sake," he answered sorrowfully, not angrily.

"Can you really pardon him?" cried Mercy, wondering, yet touched by the words.

"I can. He will be sorry one day, perhaps; at any rate, he did what he thought his duty, and war makes brutes of us all sometimes, I fear. I'd like to say good-by; but he's asleep after a weary day, so don't wake him. Tell him I'm glad *he* is to live, and that I forgive him heartily."

Although uttered between long pauses, these words seemed to have exhausted Murry, and he spoke no more till Dr. Fitz Hugh came. To him he feebly returned thanks, and whispered his farewell—then sank into a stupor, during which life ebbed fast. Both nurse and doctor forgot Clay as they hung over Murry, and neither saw the strange intentness of his face, the half awe-struck, half remorseful look he bent upon the dying man.

As the sun rose, sending in its ruddy beams across the silent ward, Murry looked up and smiled, for the bright ray fell athwart the two coats hanging on the wall beside him. Some passerby had brushed one sleeve of the blue coat across the gray, as if the inanimate things were shaking hands.

"It should be so—love our enemies; we should be brothers," he murmured faintly; and, with the last impulse of a noble nature, stretched his hand toward the man who had murdered him.

But Clay shrunk back, and covered his face without a word. When he ventured to look up, Murry was no longer there. A pale, peaceful figure lay on the narrow bed, and Mercy was smoothing the brown locks as she cut a curl for Mary and herself. Clay could not take his eyes away; as if fascinated by its serenity, he watched the dead face with gloomy eyes, till Mercy, having done her part, stopped and kissed the cold lips tenderly as she left him to his sleep. Then, as if afraid to be alone with the dead, he bid Ben put the screen between the beds, and bring him a book. His order was obeyed, but he never turned the pages, and lay with muffled head trying to shut out little Watts' sobs, as the wounded drummer-boy mourned for Murry.

Death, in a hospital, makes no stir, and in an hour no trace of the departed remained but the coat upon the wall, for Ben would not take it down, though it was his now. The empty bed stood freshly made, the clean cup and worn Bible lay ready for other hands, and the card at the bed's head hung blank for a new-comer's name. In the hurry of this event, Clay's attempted crime was forgotten for a time. But that evening Dr. Fitz Hugh told Mercy that her suspicions were correct, for the water *was* poisoned.

"How horrible! What shall we do?" she cried, with a gesture full of energetic indignation.

"Leave him to remorse," replied the doctor, sternly. "I've thought over the matter, and believe this to be the only thing we can do. I fancy the man won't live a week; his leg is in a bad way, and he is such a fiery devil, he gives himself no chance. Let him believe he killed poor Murry, at least for a few days. He thinks so now, and tries to rejoice; but if he has a human heart, he will repent."

"But he may not. Should we not tell of this? Can he not be punished?"

"Law won't hang a dying man, and I'll not denounce him. Let remorse punish him while he lives, and God judge him when he dies. Murry pardoned him; can we do less?"

Mercy's indignant face softened at the name, and for Murry's sake she yielded. Neither spoke of what they tried to think the act of a half-delirious man; and soon they could not refuse to pity him, for the doctor's prophecy proved true.

Clay was a haunted man, and remorse gnawed like a worm at his heart. Day and night he saw that tranquil face on the pillow opposite; day and night he saw the pale hand outstretched to him; day and night he heard the faint voice murmuring kindly, regretfully, "I forgive him; but I wish he had spared me, for Mary's sake."

As the days passed, and his strength visibly declined, he began to suspect that he must soon follow Murry. No one told him; for, though both doctor and nurse did their duty faithfully, neither lingered long at his bedside, and not one of the men showed any interest in him. No new patient occupied the other bed, and he lay alone in the recess with his own gloomy thoughts.

"It will be all up with me in a few days, won't it?" he asked abruptly, as Ben made his toilet one morning with unusual care, and such visible pity in his rough face that Clay could not but observe it.

"I heard the doctor say you wouldn't suffer much more. Is there any one you'd like to see, or leave a message for?" answered Ben, smoothing the long locks as gently as a woman.

"There isn't a soul in the world that cares whether I live or die, except the man who wants my money," said Clay, bitterly as his dark face grew a shade paler at this confirmation of his fear.

"Can't you head him off some way, and leave your money to some one that's been kind to you? Here's the doctor—or, better still, Miss Carrol. Neither on 'em is rich, and both on 'em has been good friends to you, or you'd 'a' fared a deal wus than you have," said Ben, not without the hope that, in saying a good word for them, he might say one for himself also.

Clay lay thinking for a moment as his face clouded over, and then brightened again.

"Miss Mercy wouldn't take it, nor the doctor either; but I know who will, and by G-d, I'll do it!" he exclaimed, with sudden energy.

His eye happened to rest on Ben as he spoke, and, feeling sure that he was to be the heir, Ben retired to send Miss Mercy, that the matter might be settled before Clay's mood changed. Miss Carrol came, and began to cut the buttons off Murry's coat while she waited for Clay to speak.

"What's that for?" he asked, restlessly.

"The men want them, and Ben is willing, for the coat is very old and ragged, you see. Murry gave his good one away to a sicker comrade, and took this instead. It was like him—my poor boy!"

"I'd like to speak to you, if you have a minute to spare," began Clay, after a pause, during which he watched her with a wistful, almost tender expression unseen by her.

"I have time; what can I do for you?" Very gentle was Mercy's voice, very pitiful her glance, as she sat down by him, for the change in his manner, and the thought of his approaching death, touched her heart.

Trying to resume his former gruffness, and cold facial expression, Clay said, as he picked nervously at the blanket,

"I've a little property that I put into the care of a friend going North. He's kept it safe; and now, as I'll never want it myself, I'd like to leave it to—" He paused an instant, glanced quickly at Mercy's face, and seeing only womanly compassion there, added with an irrepressible tremble in his voice—"to little Mary."

If he had expected any reward for the act, any comfort for his lonely death-bed, he received both in fullest measure when he saw Mercy's beautiful face flush with surprise and pleasure, her eyes fill with sudden tears, and heard her cordial voice, as she pressed his hand warmly in her own.

"I wish I could tell you how glad I am for this! I thought you were better than you seemed; I was sure you had both heart and conscience, and that you would repent before you died."

"Repent of what?" he asked, with a startled look.

"Need I tell you?" and her eye went from the empty bed to his face.

"You mean that shot? But it was only fair, after all; we killed each other, and war is nothing but wholesale murder, any way." He spoke easily, but his eyes were full of trouble, and other words seemed to tremble on his lips.

Leaning nearer, Mercy whispered in his ear,

"I mean the other murder, which you would have committed when you poisoned the cup of water he offered you, his enemy."

Every vestige of color faded out of Clay's thin face, and his haggard eyes seemed fascinated by some spectre opposite, as he muttered slowly.

"How do you know?"

"I saw you;" and she told him all the truth.

A look of intense relief passed over Clay's countenance, and the remorseful shadow lifted as he murmured brokenly,

"Thank God, I didn't kill him! Now, dying isn't so hard; now I can have a little peace."

Neither spoke for several minutes; Mercy had no words for such a time, and Clay forgot her presence as the tears dropped from between the wasted fingers spread before his face.

Presently he looked up, saying eagerly, as if his fluttering breath and rapidly failing strength warned him of approaching death,

"Will you write down a few words for me, so Mary can have the money? She needn't know any thing about me, only that I was one to whom Murry was kind, and so I gave her all I had."

"I'll get my pen and paper; rest, now, my poor fellow," said Mercy, wiping the unheeded tears away for him.

"How good it seems to hear you speak so to *me*! How can you do it?" he whispered, with such grateful wonder in his dim eyes that Mercy's heart smote her for the past.

"I do it for Murry's sake, and because I sincerely pity you."

Timidly turning his lips to kind hand, he kissed it, and then hid his face in his pillow. When Mercy returned, she observed that there were but seven tarnished buttons where she had left eight. She guessed who had taken it, but said nothing, and endeavored to render poor Clay's last hours as happy as sympathy and care could make them. The letter and will were prepared as well as they could be, and none too soon; for, as if that secret was the burden that bound Clay's spirit to the shattered body, no sooner was it lifted off, that the diviner part seemed ready to be gone.

"You'll stay with me; you'll help me die; and—oh, if I dared to ask it, I'd beg you to kiss me once when I am dead, as you did Murry. I think I could rest then, and be fitter to meet him, if the Lord lets me," he cried imploringly, as the last night gathered around him, and the coming change seemed awful to a soul that possessed no inward peace, and no firm hope to lean on through the valley of the shadow.

"I will—I will! Hold fast to me, and believe in the eternal mercy of God," whispered Miss Carrol, with her firm hand in his, her tender face bending over him as the long struggle began.

"Mercy," he murmured, catching that word, and smiling feebly as he repeated it lingeringly. "Mercy! yes, I believe in her; she'll save me, if any one can. Lord, bless and keep her forever and forever."

There was no morning sunshine to gladden his dim eyes as they looked their last, but the pale glimmer of the lamp shone full on the blue and the gray coats hanging side by side. As if the sight recalled that other death-bed, that last act of brotherly love and pardon, Clay rose up in his bed, and, while one hand clutched the button hidden in his breast, the other was outstretched toward the empty bed, as his last breath parted in a cry of remorseful longing,

"I will! I will! Forgive me, Murry, and let me say good-by!"

At Chancellorsville
The Battle of the Wilderness

Andrew Hudgins

He was an Indiana corporal
shot in the thigh when their line broke
in animal disarray. He'd crawled
into the shade and bled to death.
My uniform was shabby with
continuous wear, worn down to threads
by the inside friction of my flesh on cloth.
The armpit seams were rotted through
and almost half the buttons had dropped off.
My brother said I should remove
the Yank's clean shirt: "From now on, Sid,
he'll have no use for it." Imagining
the slack flesh shifting underneath
my hands, the other-person stink
of that man's shirt, so newly his,
I cursed Clifford from his eyeballs to
his feet. I'd never talked that way before
and didn't know I could. When we returned,
someone had beat me to the shirt.
So I had compromised my soul
for nothing I would want to use—
some knowledge I could do without.
Clifford, thank God, just laughed. It was good
stout wool, unmarked by blood.
By autumn, we wore so much blue
we could have passed for New York infantry.

THE BATTLE OF CHANCELLORSVILLE
painted 1865 Frederick A. Chapman

Stonewall Jackson

Field Notes

Battle: Chancellorsville

Location: Chancellorsville, Virginia

Date: May 1-5, 1863

Commanding Officers:

    Confederate Robert E. Lee, Stonewall Jackson

    Union "Fighting Joe" Hooker, George Gordon Meade

Behind the lines: Stonewall Jackson was shot by friendly fire, and died of his wounds six days later.

Winner: Confederacy

Lee Surrenders to Grant

April 9, 1865
Appomattox Court House, Virginia

Horace Porter

Grant had trapped Lee near Appomattox Court House, Virginia, after relentlessly chasing the Confederate army for weeks. Lee and Grant sought a surrender that would end the war and benefit the soldiers of both sides. Eyewitness Horace Porter was Grant's aide-de-camp.

General Grant began the conversation by saying: "I met you once before, General Lee, while we were serving in Mexico, when you came over from General [Winfield] Scott's headquarters to visit Garlands' brigade, to which I then belonged. I have always remembered your appearance, and I think I should have recognized you anywhere." "Yes," replied General Lee, "I know I met you on that occasion, and I have often thought of it and tried to recollect how you looked, but I have never been able to recall a single feature." After some further mention of Mexico, General Lee said: "I suppose, General Grant, that the object of our present meeting is fully understood. I asked to see you to ascertain upon what terms you would receive the surrender of my army." General Grant replied: "The terms I propose are those stated substantially in my letter of yesterday—that is, the officers and men surrendered to be paroled and disqualified from taking up arms again until properly exchanged, and all arms, ammunition, and supplies to be delivered up as captured property." Lee nodded an assent,[1] and said: "Those are about the conditions which I expected would be proposed." General

1 **assent:** agreement

Grant then continued: "Yes, I think our correspondence indicated pretty clearly the action that would be taken at our meeting; and I hope it may lead to a general suspension of hostilities and be the means of preventing any further loss of life."

Lee inclined his head as indicating his accord with this wish, and General Grant then went on to talk at some length in a very pleasant vein about the prospects of peace. Lee was evidently anxious to proceed to the formal work of the surrender, and he brought the subject up again by saying:

"I presume, General Grant, we have both carefully considered the proper steps to be taken, and I would suggest that you commit to writing the terms you have proposed, so that they may be formally acted upon."

"Very well," replied General Grant, "I will write them out." And calling for his manifold order-book, he opened it on the table before him and proceeded to write the terms. The leaves had been so prepared that three impressions of the writing were made. He wrote very rapidly, and did not pause until he had finished the sentence ending with "officers appointed by me to receive them." Then he looked toward Lee, and his eyes seemed to be resting on the handsome sword that hung at that officer's side. He said afterward that this set him to thinking that it would be an unnecessary humiliation to require the officers to surrender their swords, and a great hardship to deprive them of their personal baggage and horses, and after a short pause he wrote the sentence: "This will not embrace the side-arms of the officers, nor their private horses or baggage." . . . When this had been done, he handed the book to General Lee and asked him to read over the letter. . . .

. . . When Lee came to the sentence about the officers' side-arms, private horses, and baggage, he showed for the first time during the reading of the letter a slight change of countenance,[2] and was evidently touched by this act of generosity. It was doubtless the condition mentioned to which he particularly alluded when he looked toward General Grant as he finished reading and said with some degree of warmth in his manner: "This will have a very happy effect upon my army."

General Grant then said: "Unless you have some suggestions to make in regard to the form in which I have stated the terms, I will have a copy of the letter made in ink and sign it."

"There is one thing I would like to mention," Lee replied after a short pause. "The cavalrymen and artillerists own their own horses in our

2 countenance: expression

army. Its organization in this respect differs from that of the United States." This expression attracted the notice of our officers present, as showing how firmly the conviction was grounded in his mind that we were two distinct countries. He continued: "I would like to understand whether these men will be permitted to retain their horses?"

"You will find that the terms as written do not allow this," General Grant replied; "only the officers are permitted to take their private property."

Lee read over the second page of the letter again, and then said:

"No, I see the terms do not allow it; that is clear." His face showed plainly that he was quite anxious to have this concession made, and Grant said very promptly and without giving Lee time to make a direct request:

"Well, the subject is quite new to me. Of course I did not know that any private soldiers owned their animals, but I think this will be the last battle of the war—I sincerely hope so—and that the surrender of this army will be followed soon by that of all the others, and I take it that most of the men in the ranks are small farmers, and as the country has been so raided by the two armies, it is doubtful whether they will be able to put in a crop to carry themselves and their families through the next winter without the aid of the horses they are now riding, and I will arrange it in this way: I will not change the terms as now written, but I will instruct the officers I shall appoint to receive the paroles to let all the men who claim to own a horse or mule take the animals home

SURRENDER AT APPOMATTOX

painted 1869
Thomas Lovell

with them to work their little farms." (This expression has been quoted in various forms and has been the subject of some dispute. I give the exact words used.) . . .

. . . General Lee now took the initiative again in leading the conversation back into business channels. He said:

"I have a thousand or more of your men as prisoners, General Grant, a number of them officers whom we have required to march along with us for several days. I shall be glad to send them into your lines as soon as it can be arranged, for I have no provisions[3] for them. I have, indeed, nothing for my own men. They have been living for the last few days principally upon parched corn, and we are badly in need of both rations and forage[4]. . . ."

. . . General Grant replied: "I should like to have our men sent within our lines as soon as possible. I will take steps at once to have your army supplied with rations, but I am sorry we have no forage for the animals." . . .

. . . At a little before 4 o'clock General Lee shook hands with General Grant, bowed to the other officers, and with Colonel Marshall left the room. One after another we followed, and passed out to the porch. Lee signaled to his orderly to bring up his horse, and while the animal was being bridled the general stood on the lowest step and gazed sadly in the direction of the valley beyond where his army lay—now an army of prisoners. He smote[5] his hands together a number of times in an absent sort of a way; seemed not to see the group of Union officers in the yard who rose respectfully at his approach, and appeared unconscious of everything about him. All appreciated the sadness that overwhelmed him, and he had the personal sympathy of every one who beheld him at this supreme moment of trial. The approach of his horse seemed to recall him from his reverie, and he at once mounted. General Grant now stepped down from the porch, and, moving toward him, saluted him by raising his hat. He was followed in this act of courtesy by all our officers present; Lee raised his hat respectfully, and rode off to break the sad news to the brave fellows whom he had so long commanded. ⨍

---

3 **provisions:** food or supplies

4 **forage:** food for animals

5 **smote:** struck

Farewell Order to the Army of Northern Virginia

After four years of arduous service, marked by unsurpassed courage and fortitude, the Army of Northern Virginia has been compelled to yield to overwhelming numbers and resources. I need not tell the survivors of so many hard-fought battles, who have remained steadfast to the last, that I consented to this result from no distrust of them; but feeling that valor and devotion could accomplish nothing that would compensate for the loss that would have attended the continuation of the contest, I determined to avoid the useless sacrifice of those whose past services have endeared them to their countrymen.

By the terms of the agreement, officers and men can return to their homes and remain there until exchanged. You will take with you the satisfaction that proceeds from the consciousness of duty faithfully performed; and I earnestly pray that a merciful God will extend to you His blessing and protection.

With an increasing admiration of your constancy and devotion to your country, and a grateful remembrance of your kind and generous consideration of myself, I bid you an affectionate farewell.

Robert E. Lee

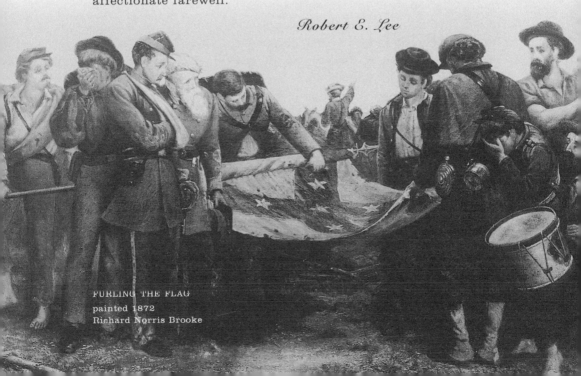

FURLING THE FLAG
painted 1872
Richard Norris Brooke

Death of Lincoln

April 14-15, 1865

Washington, D.C.

Gideon Welles

Five days after Lee's surrender, President Lincoln decided to take an
evening's rest at the play "Our American Cousin" at nearby Ford's
Theatre. There, an actor with Southern sympathies leapt into
the President's box and shot him. Lincoln died on Good Friday, 1865.
Welles was Lincoln's secretary of the Navy.

April 14

General Grant was present at the meeting of the Cabinet to-day and
remained during the session.

Inquiry had been made as to army news and especially if any information have been received from Sherman.[1] None of the members had
heard anything, and Stanton, who makes it a point to be late, and who
has the telegraph in his department, had not arrived.

General Grant said he was hourly expecting word. The President
remarked, it would, he had no doubt, come soon, and come favorable,
for he had last night the usual dream which he had preceding nearly
every great and important event of the War. Generally the news had been
favorable which succeeded this dream, and the dream itself was always
the same.

I inquired what this remarkable dream could be. He said it related to
your (my) element, the water; that he seemed to be in some singular,
indescribable vessel, and that he was moving with great rapidity towards
an indefinite shore; that he had this dream preceding Sumter, Bull Run,
Antietam, Gettysburg, Stone River, Vicksburg, Wilmington, etc.

1 At this point, General William T. Sherman was still fighting the
Confederate army led by General Joseph Johnston.

"I had," the President remarked, "this strange dream again last night, and we shall, judging from the past, have great news very soon."

I write this conversation three days after it occurred, in consequence of what took place Friday night, and but for which the mention of this dream would probably have never been noted. Great events did, indeed, follow, for within a few hours the good and gentle, as well as truly great, man who narrated his dream closed forever his earthly career.

I had retired to bed about half past ten on the evening of the 14th of April, and was just getting asleep when Mrs. Welles, my wife, said some one was at our door. Sitting up in bed, I heard a voice twice call to John, my son, whose sleeping-room was on the second floor directly over the front entrance.

I arose at once and raised a window, when my messenger, James Smith, called to me that Mr. Lincoln, the President, had been shot, and said Secretary Seward and his son, Assistant Secretary Frederick Seward, were assassinated.[2]

James was much alarmed and excited. I told him his story was incoherent and improbable, that he was associating men who were not together and

2 **Seward and his son . . . :** Both were shot by an accomplice of John Wilkes Booth.

liable to attack at the same time. "Where," I inquired, "was the President when shot?" James said he was at Ford's Theatre on 10th Street. "Well," said I, "Secretary Seward is an invalid in bed in his house on 15th Street."

James said he had been there, stopped in at the house to make inquiry before alarming me.

I immediately dressed myself, and, against the earnest remonstrance and appeals of my wife, went directly to Mr. Seward's, whose residence was on the east side of the square, mine being on the north. James accompanied me.

As we were crossing 15th Street I saw four or five men in earnest consultation, standing under the lamp on the corner by St. John's Church. Before I had got half across the street, the lamp was suddenly extinguished and the knot of persons rapidly dispersed. For a moment, and but a moment, I was disconcerted to find myself in darkness, but, recollecting that it was late and about time for the moon to rise, I proceeded. Hurrying forward into 15th Street, I found it pretty full of people, especially near the residence of Secretary Seward.

Entering the house, I found the lower hall and office full of persons, and among them most of the foreign legations, all anxiously inquiring what truth there was in the horrible rumors afloat.

Proceeding through the hall to the stairs, I found one and I think two of the servants there holding the crowd in check. The servants were frightened and appeared relieved to see me.

I asked for the Secretary's room and proceeded to the foot of the bed. Dr. Verdi and, I think, two others were there. The bed was saturated with blood. The Secretary was lying on his back, the upper part of his head covered by a cloth, which extends down over his eyes. His mouth was open, the lower jaw dropping down.

I exchanged a few whispered words with Dr. V. Secretary Stanton, who came after but almost simultaneously with me, made inquiries in a louder tone till admonished by a word from one of the physicians. We almost immediately withdrew and went into the adjoining front room, where lay Frederick Seward. His eyes were open but he did not move them, nor a limb, nor did he speak. Doctor White, who was in attendance, told me he was unconscious and more dangerously injured than his father.

As we descended the stairs, I asked Stanton what he had heard in regard to the President that was reliable. He said the President was shot at Ford's Theatre, that he had seen a man who was present and witnessed the occurrence.

The streets were full of people. Not only the sidewalk but the carriage-way was to some extent occupied, all or nearly all hurrying towards 10th Street. When we entered the street we found it pretty closely packed.

The President had been carried across the street from the theatre to the house of a Mr. Peterson. We entered by ascending a flight of steps above the basement and passing through a long hall to the rear, where the President lay, extended on a bed, breathing heavily.

Several surgeons were present, at least six, I should think more. Among them I was glad to observe Dr. Hall, who, however, soon left. I inquired of Dr. H. as I entered the true condition of the President. He replied the President was dead to all intents, although he might live three hours or perhaps longer.

The giant sufferer lay extended diagonally across the bed, which was not long enough for him. He had been stripped of his clothes. His large arms, which were occasionally exposed, were of a size which one would scarce have expected from his spare appearance. His slow, full respiration lifted the clothes with each breath that he took. His features were calm and striking. I had never seen them appear to better advantage than for the first hour, perhaps, that I was there. After that, his right eye began to swell and that part of his face became discolored.

Senator Sumner was there, I think, when I entered. If not he came in soon after, as did Speaker Colfax, Mr. Secretary McCulloch, and the other members of the Cabinet, with the exception of Mr. Seward.

A double guard was stationed at the door and on the sidewalk, to repress the crowd, which was of course highly excited and anxious.

The room was small and overcrowded. The surgeons and members of the Cabinet were as many as should have been in the room, but there were many more, and the hall and other rooms in the front or main house were full. One of these rooms was occupied by Mrs. Lincoln and her attendants, with Miss Harris. About once an hour Mrs. Lincoln would repair to the bedside of her dying husband and with lamentation and tears remain until overcome by emotion.

April 15

A door which opened upon a porch or gallery, and also the windows, were kept open for fresh air. The night was dark, cloudy and damp, and about six it began to rain. I remained in the room until then without sitting or leaving it, when, there being a vacant chair which some one left at the foot of the bed, I occupied it for nearly two hours, listening to the heavy groans, and witnessing the wasting life of the good and great man who was expiring before me.

About 6 a.m. I experienced a feeling of faintness and for the first time after entering the room, a little past eleven, I left it and the house and took a short walk in the open air. It was a dark and gloomy morning, and rain set in before I returned to the house, some fifteen minutes later.

Large groups of people were gathered every few rods, all anxious and solicitous. Some one or more from each group stepped forward as I passed, to inquire into the condition of the President, and to ask if there was no hope. Intense grief was on every countenance when I replied that the President could survive but a short time. The colored people especially—

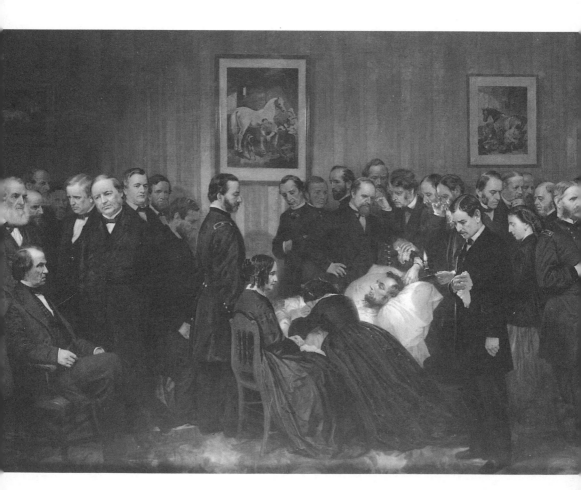

and there were at this time more of them, perhaps, than of whites—were overwhelmed with grief.

Returning to the house, I seated myself in the back parlor, where the Attorney General and others had been engaged in taking evidence concerning the assassination.

A little before seven, I went into the room where the dying President was rapidly drawing near the closing moments. His wife soon after made her last visit to him. The death-struggle had begun. Robert, his son, stood with several others at the head of the bed. He bore himself well, but on two occasions gave way to overpowering grief and sobbed aloud, turning his head and leaning on the shoulder of Senator Sumner.

The respiration of the President became suspended at intervals, and at last entirely ceased at twenty-two minutes past seven.

A prayer followed from Dr. Gurley, and the Cabinet, with the exception of Mr. Seward and Mr. McCulloch, immediately thereafter assembled in the back parlor, from which all other persons were excluded, and there signed a letter which was prepared by Attorney General Speed to the Vice-President, informing him of the event, and that the government devolved upon him.

I went after breakfast to the Executive Mansion. There was a cheerless cold rain and everything seemed gloomy. On the Avenue in front of the White House were several hundred colored people, mostly women and children, weeping and wailing their loss. This crowd did not appear to diminish through the whole of that cold wet day. They seemed not to know what was to be their fate since their great benefactor was dead, and their hopeless grief affected me more than almost anything else, though strong and brave men wept when I met them.

At the White House all was silent and sad. As we were descending the stairs, "Tad," who was looking from the window at the foot, turned and, seeing us, cried aloud in his tears, "Oh, Mr. Welles, who killed my father?"

THE LAST HOURS OF LINCOLN
painted 1868   Alonzo Chappel

RESPONDING TO CLUSTER THREE

WHAT WERE THE COSTS OF THE WAR?

Thinking Skill SUMMARIZING

1. The cost of the war was high in dollars and lives lost for both sides. It was also costly on a personal level. Evaluate what was sacrificed by three of the characters or historical figures you have read about so far. You might want to use a chart such as the one below in which an example has been done for you.

Individual	What was sacrificed	What, if anything, was gained by the sacrifice
Clay in "The Blue and the Gray"	He sacrificed his pride	He gained peace of mind

2. The poem "At Chancellorsville" is told from the viewpoint of a Confederate soldier shortly after the Battle of the Wilderness, which was fought in May of 1863. List some of the details from the poem that show the living conditions of soldiers in the Confederate army.

3. Louisa May Alcott uses **symbolism** in her short story "The Blue and the Gray." A *symbol* is an object, a person, an animal, a color, or other device that stands for a more abstract concept. For example, an eagle sometimes stands for freedom; the color green sometimes signifies growth. What symbols does Alcott use in her short story, and what do you think they signify?

4. Even in defeat, General Lee's gracious attitude can be seen in both the account of his surrender and his farewell speech. Find three phrases or events in these two selections that reveal his character.

Writing Activity: Summarizing the Civil War

Imagine you are trying to describe the American Civil War to someone from another country. Write three to five statements that **summarize** this period in U.S. history. You might address the following issues in your summary statements: the main causes, the costs of the war, how the conflict was resolved, and the effects of the war.

To Summarize

- restate facts and concepts in your own words
- emphasize important events and figures
- avoid story-telling terms such as "and then" and "next"

CLUSTER FOUR

Thinking on Your Own

Thinking Skill SYNTHESIZING

K.K.Klan Ala 1868

Petition from Kentucky Citizens on Ku Klux Klan Violence

African Americans were freed by Lincoln's Emancipation Proclamation, but they suffered from almost constant persecution in the South. Laws were passed limiting their right to vote, own property, and seek education. A group of former Confederate soldiers created a social club, the Ku Klux Klan. The Klan later became famous for their "night rides" throughout the South, terrorizing black citizens.

This is one letter documenting the harassment experienced by blacks in the area surrounding Frankfort, Kentucky, from 1867-1871.

To the Senate and House of Representative in Congress assembled: We the Colored Citizens of Frankfort and vicinity do this day memorialize your honorable bodies upon the condition of affairs now existing in this the state of Kentucky.

We would respectfully state that life, liberty and property are unprotected among the colored race of this state. Organized Bands of desperate and lawless men mainly composed of soldiers of the late Rebel Armies Armed disciplined and disguised and bound by Oath and secret obligations have by force terror and violence subverted all civil society among Colored people, thus utterly rendering insecure the safety of persons and property, overthrowing all those rights which are the primary basis and objects of the Government which are expressly guaranteed to us by the Constitution of the United States as amended; We believe you are not familiar with the description of the Ku Klux Klans riding nightly over the country going from County to County and in the County towns spreading terror wherever they go, by robbing whipping ravishing and killing our people without provocation, compelling Colored people to brake the ice and bathe in the Chilly waters of the Kentucky River.

The Legislature has adjourned they refused to enact any laws to suppress Ku Klux disorder. We regard them as now being licensed to continue their dark and bloody deeds under cover of the dark night. They refuse to allow us to testify in the state Courts where a white man is concerned. We find their deeds are perpetrated only upon Colored men and white Republicans. We also find that for our services to the Government and our race we have become the special object of hatred and persecution at the hands of the Democratic party. Our people are driven from their homes in great numbers having no redress only the U.S. Courts which is in many cases unable to reach them. We would state

Colored schoolhouse burned, 1867.

that we have been law abiding citizens, pay our tax and in many parts of the state our people have been driven from the poles refused the right to vote. Many have been slaughtered while attempting to vote, we ask how long is this state of things to last.

We appeal to you as law abiding citizens to enact some laws that will protects us. And that will enable us to exercise the rights of citizens. We see desperaders in the state, for information, we lay before you an number of violent acts occured during his Administration. Although he Stevenson says half Dozen instances of violence did occur these are not more than one half the acts that have occured. They Democratic party has here a political organization composed only of Democrats not a single Republican can join them where many of these acts have been committed it has been proven that they were the men, don with Armies from the State Arsenal. We pray you will take some steps to remedy these evils.

Done by a Committee of Grievances appointed at a meeting of all the Colored Citizens of Frankfort & vicinity.

Mar. 25th, 1871

Henry Marrs, *Teacher colored school*

Henry Lynn, *Livery stable keeper*

N.N. Trumbo, *Grocer*

Samuel Damsey, *B. Smith [Blacksmith]*

B.T. Crampton, *Barber*

PETITION

1. A mob visited Harrodsburg in Mercer County to take from jail a man name Robertson, Nov. 14, 1867.

2. Smith attacked and whipped by regulation in Zelun County Nov. 1867.

3. Colored school house burned by incendiaries in Breckinridge Dec. 24, 1867.

4. A Negro Jim Macklin taken from jail in Frankfort and hung by mob January 28, 1868.

5. Sam Davis hung by mob in Harrodsburg May 28, 1868.

6. Wm. Pierce hung by a mob in Christian July 12, 1868.

7. Geo. Roger hung by a mob in Bradsfordsville Martin County July 11, 1868.

8. Colored school Exhibition at Midway attacked by a mob July 31, 1868.

9. Seven person ordered to leave their homes at Standford, Ky. Aug. 7, 1868.

10. Silas Woodford age sixty badly beaten by disguised mob. Mary Smith Curtis and Margaret Mosby also badly beaten, near Keene Jessemine County Aug. 1868.

11. Cabe Fields shot — and killed by disguise men near Keene Jessamine County Aug. 3, 1868.

12. James Gaines expelled from Anderson by Ku Klux Aug. 1868.

13. James Parker killed by Ku Klux Pulaski, Aug. 1868.

14. Noah Blakenship whipped by a mob in Pulaski County Aug. 1868.

15. Negroes attacked robbed and driven from Summerville in Green County Aug. 21, 1868.

16. William Gibson and John Gibson hung by a mob in Washington County Aug. 1868.

17. F.H. Montford hung by an mob near Cogers landing in Jessamine County Aug. 28, 1868.

18. Wm. Glassgow killed by a mob in Warren County Sep. 5, 1868.

19. Negro hung by a mob Sep. 1868.

★   ★   ★   ★   ★   ★

110. Negro church & school house in Scott county [burned?] Jan. 13, 1871.

111. Ku Klux maltreated Demar his two sons and Joseph Allen in Franklin Jan. 1871.

112. Dr Johnson whipped by Ku Klux in Magoffin county Dec. 1871.

113. Property burned by incendiaries in Fayette county Jan. 21, 1871.

114. Attack on mail agent — North Benson Jan. 26, 1871.

115. Winston Hawkins fence burned and notice over his door not come home any more April 2d, 1871.

116. Ku Klux to the number of two hundred in February came into Frankfort and rescued from jail one Scroggins that was in civil custody for shooting and killing one colored man named Steader Trumbo.

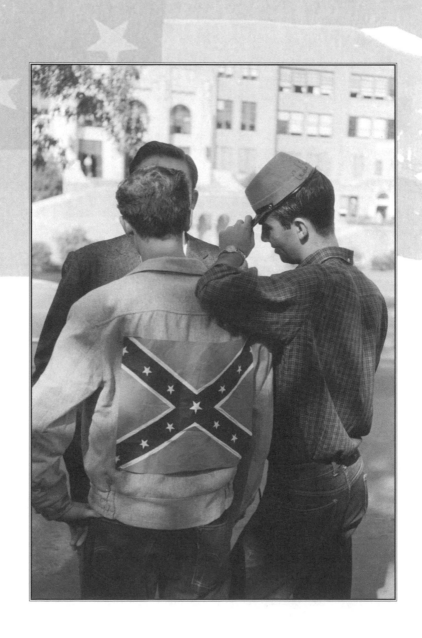

Still a Shooting War

FROM *Confederates in the Attic*

Tony Horwitz

The mystery began with the circumstances surrounding Michael Westerman's death. Westerman and his wife, Hannah, had been high school sweethearts, about to enjoy their first night out since the birth of their twins five weeks before. They planned to buy Hannah a denim dress before going to dinner in Nashville, an hour south of Guthrie. En route, at about four o'clock, Michael stopped for gas at a convenience store called Janie's Market, on Guthrie's main street.

Westerman's truck caught the eye of four black teenagers who were parked in a car nearby. The pickup was hard to miss: a big red Chevy 4x4 with a jacked-up chassis, a rebel-flag license plate, and a large rebel flag flapping from a pole in the truck's bed. The car's driver, Damien Darden, thought he'd seen the flag-waving truck before, cruising through Guthrie's black neighborhood.

"Let's go whip that dude," he told his friends, speeding off to recruit others for the brawl. Because the Westermans' truck had dark tinted windows, Darden and his friends couldn't see that the pair inside were former neighbors and classmates.

Michael Westerman pumped gas and bought watermelon bubble gum, then sat chatting in the cab with Hannah. The two weren't in any hurry. They'd left the twins with Michael's parents and had the whole evening to themselves.

Damien Darden returned to Janie's Market trailed by two other cars, and pulled alongside the pickup. Several of the black teenagers later testified that a white hand reached out the truck's sliding back window and shook the rebel flag. One of them said he heard someone in the truck shout "N—s!" Hannah denied that she or Michael had said or done anything.

Michael pulled out of Janie's and drove south into Tennessee. Hannah glanced back and saw the three cars from Janie's trailing behind. "Kick it!" she said, and Michael floored the accelerator, hurtling down the two-lane highway.

At about the same moment, in the backseat of Darden's car, a seventeen-year-old named Freddie Morrow told his friends he had a gun. "No you don't," the others taunted. Freddie reached inside his belt and brandished a cheap .32 pistol. Damien Darden sped up, gaining ground on the flag-bearing truck.

A few miles south of Guthrie, near a forlorn railroad siding, Freddie fired wildly out the window. Then the gun jammed. Damien accelerated and pulled into the oncoming lane. He and Michael now raced side by side going eighty-five. Michael shoved Hannah to the floor. Freddie unjammed his gun, stuck his hand out the window and fired again.

Hannah didn't hear the blast but she saw her husband clutch his side and moan, "Oh my God, they shot me." As the truck slowed, she somehow scrambled over Michael into the driver's seat. Damien's car had stopped in the road just ahead; another car from Janie's pulled up behind the pickup. Hannah thought the cars were trying to box her in. So she swerved off the road, did a U-turn, and sped back toward Kentucky as Freddie fired again.

By the time Hannah reached a hospital emergency room, Michael was in shock. A bullet had passed through his heart. Surgeons closed the wound and rushed him by ambulance to Nashville, where he died the next day. When police searched the Westermans' truck, they found a single bullet hole in the door, Michael's loaded .380 automatic on the floor, and his black cowboy hat with a big wad of watermelon bubble gum stuck to the brim.

* * *

The episode bristled with question marks. Who was Michael Westerman and what did he mean by flying the flag in a largely black town on Martin Luther King's birthday weekend? Why had this so provoked Damien and his friends that they chased down and killed a white man in broad daylight? And why had violent rage over the rebel flag erupted here of all places, in Warren's "un-Southern" hometown, in a state that never joined the Confederacy?

On a Sunday morning, I went looking for clues in the Todd County seat of Elkton. Located at the county's main crossroads, ten minutes north of Guthrie, Elkton was home to the high school that both the Westermans and their assailants attended. It was also here that Michael had sometimes cruised with his rebel flag, circling the courthouse square and crawling past an adjoining stretch of fast-food joints. In a dry county[1] with no mall or movie theater (or even a stoplight), looping between the Dairy Mart and the Dairy Queen provided what little action was available. Teenagers called this 1950s-style ritual "flipping the dip."

When I arrived, the dip was flipping with rebel-flag-toting trucks. There were also two cars with holes crudely drilled in their rooftops and flagpoles poking out, like mutant hair follicles. One member of this ersatz[2] color guard wore a rebel kepi[3] and carried a loaded .22 pistol in his lap. He told me he'd only begun flying the flag since Michael's death. "One goes down, two fill his space," he said. Then, flag hoisted high, he shouted "These colors don't run!" and sped off toward the Dairy Queen.

Nearby, a dozen people in jungle fatigues and combat boots stood at strategic points around the square, handing out flyers to the after-church traffic. I approached the troop's leader, a bearded man with a walkie-talkie, and asked what was up. "Literature roadblock," he said, handing me several flyers. The first was headlined: "The only Reason You are White! Today is Because Your Ancestors Practiced & Believed in Segregation YESTERDAY!" The second commanded: "I WANT YOU FOR THE ALMIGHTY KU KLUX KLAN!"

The literature was signed "Yours for White Victory, Ron Edwards, Grand Dragon for Christ, Race & Nation." This was the same bearded man who stood before me, barking un-dragonlike orders into his walkie-talkie. "Cross the street only on the crosswalks, and stay on the sidewalks!" he commanded his underlings. Then to me: "I don't want us breaking any laws."

1 **dry county:** a county in which no alcohol sales are allowed

2 **ersatz:** imitation

3 **kepi:** military cap

Passing cars honked and gave the thumbs up. Several motorists swapped church pamphlets—"What Must I Do To Be Saved?"— for the Klan's exclamatory literature: "Justice For Our People NOW!" Then a burly pedestrian in a farm cap stopped to grouse, "I've had enough of n—s telling us what to do."

The Klan handed out 750 flyers and signed up ten new acolytes[4] before melting back into the Kentucky hills, leaving Elkton Sunday-quiet. The only place open on the square was a luncheonette called the Town Grill. A petition lay on the counter: "We the undersigned believe the rebel mascot should stay at Todd County schools. We are the South, let us wave our pride." The waitress explained that Todd County Central High School called its sports teams "the Rebels" and took as its logo two flag-waving Confederates. But just before Michael Westerman's shooting, a committee of prominent citizens had quietly recommended that the school drop the rebel motif to ease racial tension.

To the waitress and many other whites, this assault on the rebel mascot by local elites, meeting behind closed doors, mirrored the assault on Westerman and his flag by angry young blacks. "They're fixin' to strip white people—whites that ain't rich—of what little they got," the waitress said.

The petition drive was led by a retired nurse named Frances Chapman. I called her from the grill to ask to come chat. En route, I stopped at Todd Central, a low-slung brick school with bright hallways and new computer labs. It looked like any other public high school, except for a vast mural in the foyer of the notorious mascot: two cartoonish Confederates clutching battle flags and blowing bugles emitting the words "Go, Rebels, Go."

I was surprised that these flabby caricatures had provoked such a storm. They seemed to mock rather than exalt the Confederacy. But Frances Chapman didn't see it that way. "The fat men, oooh, I think they're wonderful!" she exclaimed. "They make me feel so proud."

Chapman was a tiny woman with oversized glasses and an electric-green pants suit. Her words were equally arresting. As soon as I sat down, she showed me a newspaper story quoting her recent comments on a local radio show. "Slavery was not all that bad," she'd declared. "A lot of people were quite happy to be living on large plantations."

Chapman smiled sweetly. "Blacks just need to get over slavery," she said, as though talking of the flu. "You can't live in the past."

---

4 **acolytes:** assistants

I gently observed that she herself might be accused of living in the past by defending the rebel flag. "Oh no, that's about now," she said. "Blacks don't really have anything against the flag. They just don't want us to have it. They want the best jobs, the biggest money. Now they want this. If we lose the mascot, it'll just be a matter of time before we lose everything." Her voice quivered with rage. "Don't put *us* where *they* used to be."

It was the same bitterness I'd heard from Bud Sharpe, the pro-flag demonstrator in Columbia. For both Sharpe and Chapman, the rebel banner represented a finger in the dike, the last brake against a noisome[5] tide of minority rights that was fast eroding the status of whites. "The pity of it is," Chapman went on, "blacks have a great legacy. They had Ray Charles, Duke Ellington, George Washington Carver. They first learned dancing and singing—we learned that from them."

Chapman had learned something else from blacks: the idiom and tactics of civil rights. She and her supporters had launched a school boycott, with scores of white families pulling their kids out of Todd Central and threatening to withhold county taxes unless the rebel mascot was retained. They also planned a sit-in at the next school board meeting. Chapman had printed a special T-shirt for the protest, adorned with the Confederate flag and the words: SHOW RESPECT—You're in Rebel Country.

Seeing me to the door, Chapman raised her small fist above her head. "We shall overcome," she said.

* * *

The next day at Elkton's library, I learned a strange thing. Todd County wasn't rebel country, at least not historically. According to the volumes of local history I perused, most Todd Countians supported the Union in the Civil War. Like much of the upper south, the county split along geographic lines. Whites from the county's fertile plantations bordering Tennessee tended to side with the South. But the more numerous yeoman farmers in Todd County's hilly north (where slaves were few) supported the Union. Kentucky also stayed in the Union, though the first Confederate Congress optimistically allotted a star for Kentucky on the Confederacy's flag in hopes the state might secede.

Despite this history, almost all whites I spoke to echoed Frances Chapman, proclaiming their county rebel territory and believing it had

5 noisome: harmful

always been so. As proof, they pointed to a 351-foot concrete spike soaring at the county's western edge. The obelisk marked the birthsite of Confederate president Jefferson Davis, who was born there in 1808 (only a hundred miles and eight months apart from his future antagonist, Abraham Lincoln).

* * *

As Frances Chapman had promised, hundreds of people packed the bleachers of a middle-school gym for the next meeting of the Todd County school board. Some wore kepis and rebel-flag bandannas, others the "SHOW RESPECT—You're in Rebel Country" T-shirts Chapman had printed for the meeting.

A few black families sat by the exit, as did all four members of the Sheriff's Department. The school board perched around a table on the gym floor, awkwardly conducting routine business. Finally, as the crowd grew restive, a board member set up a microphone and invited the public to comment.

The first to speak was a military widow. "My husband was a Yankee and I converted him to a rebel and I'm proud of it!" she shouted. "I will not compromise my values and equal rights to satisfy a minority. God bless America, God bless our rebel flag!" She threw open her cardigan to reveal the "SHOW RESPECT" T-shirt she wore underneath. The crowd behind her roared.

Next, a lean, bleached-blonde woman strode to the microphone and jabbed her finger at the school board. "Listen to us—we put you there!" Flushed with rage, she said her son at Todd Central was forced to take off a rebel-flag T-shirt the week after Westerman's murder. Metal detectors had also been installed at the school to prevent further violence.

"They even took away my boy's pepper spray!" someone shouted from the bleachers.

"Sure ain't right!" the woman at the microphone yelled.

The crowd began stamping its feet and chanting, "Discrimination! Discrimination!" As the woman returned to her seat, she pumped her fists in the air like a prizefighter leaving the ring.

The meeting went on like this for two hours. As the twentieth or so woman spat venom at the school board, it struck me that recent media attention lavished on "angry white males" neglected the considerable depths of female rage on display here, and everywhere else I'd been in Todd County. Tonight, at least, these trailer-bound, factory-trapped women could vent their rage and affirm the race consciousness that blacks had exhibited for decades, even flashing their "RESPECT" shirts with Aretha-like[6] pride.

Frances Chapman claimed the last word. Waving her petition, which now bore 3,000 names, a quarter of the county's population, she shouted, "Don't ever count us out!" Then she and the other whites stormed from the gym and into the flurrying snow. They lingered outside, waving flags and shouting, as though vaguely dissatisfied. Neither the school board nor the few blacks at the meeting had responded.

Inside the gym, a half-dozen black women stood waiting for the parking lot to clear. "I work in Todd County," one woman said softly. "I pay my taxes and my children go to school, too. I feel like, why shouldn't we have a say about the school mascot? Kids are killing kids over this. Don't you think it's time we at least start talking about it?"

I asked why she hadn't made this sensible comment during the meeting. She looked at me as though I was crazy. "Who's listening?" she asked.

Another woman had the blank, haunted look of a shell-shocked soldier. Before Michael Westerman's death, she said, white rancor toward blacks was contained. "We were living with it. I felt like they respected us." But now she wondered if she'd been fooling herself her whole life.

6 **Aretha-like:** reference to Aretha Franklin and her song "Respect"

"That flag opens up a racial door we've been keeping closed for so many years. It's a way of saying what white people have kept bottled up."

She paused as the sound of chanting—"equal rights for whites!"—drifted through the open gym door. The woman shook her head. "They've gone loco on us," she said.

* * *

In the week following the school meeting, I made the rounds of local officials, ministers and long-time residents, searching for clues about what was happening to Todd County. From both blacks and whites came the same, bewildered refrain. Though Jim Crow hadn't been as rigid in Kentucky as it was farther South, the past three decades had witnessed extraordinary change. Blacks and whites mingled freely at schools, work-places, restaurants and other public places. Yet for reasons no one fully understood, this intimacy had spawned a subterranean rage, which had boiled over with the shooting of Michael Westerman and the tumult following his death.

"We're a little ol' Southern Mayberry," Guthrie's mayor told me. "Or I thought we were." A portly man of thirty-six, he'd campaigned for mayor of the town of 1,600 with the slogan "I'm a good guy and will work hard for you." I found him fastidiously sweeping Guthrie's diminutive town hall. "When I was a boy, no one cared about that flag," he went on. "Heck, I never even thought of myself as Southern. But today there's this intolerance, white and black. People feel they have to wave their beliefs in each other's faces."

A few blocks away, a middle-aged black storekeeper echoed the mayor's words. "Kids today, they're weaker and wiser," she said, sifting turnip greens and smoking Kools. "A lot of things we didn't pay attention to, they do. If we were called n—r, we shook it off. Just went about our business. Not now. It's strange, my kids have white friends, which I never did. But they got white enemies, too."

Michael Westerman's brief life seemed to typify this paradox. He grew up on the same street of modest brick ranch homes as two of the black youths who would later be charged with his murder. They went to the same schools and shot hoops in the Westermans' driveway. Michael's father, a tenant farmer, served on the volunteer fire department with relatives of the black teenagers. Michael's mother ran a sewing machine at Guthrie Garment, a plant whose workforce was evenly divided between black and white. At Todd Central, interracial dating had become common. A few months before Michael's death, a black student was voted Homecoming Queen over several white competitors.

But amid this apparent racial amity, a low-grade guerrilla war brewed between some blacks and whites. Earlier generations of blacks in Todd County had quietly endured exaltation of Jeff Davis, the rebel flag, and the defunct nation for which it stood. Black athletes at Todd Central dribbled basketballs across a gym floor painted with the school's rebel mascot; they wore class rings decorated with rebel emblems; they bought the "Rebel" yearbook, which for many years included a photo of two students annually anointed "The General and His Southern Lady" and pictured in hoop skirt and Confederate uniform.

"Back then, parents told you to sit your butt down, work hard and keep your mouth shut around white people," said Kim Gardner, a Todd Central student in the late 1970s. I was visiting Gardner at her trailer outside Elkton. Her daughter Shanekia, a junior at Todd Central, sat beside her mother in tight jeans and Timberland boots, beneath a poster of Malcolm X. As I spoke with Kim, Shanekia shook her head. "We aren't going to just take it like our parents did," she said. "I keep telling Momma times has changed."

* * *

Times had changed across the South, and in some ways Todd County was just catching up. Though black hostility to Confederate totems lay relatively dormant for two decades after the civil rights struggles of the early 1960s, it resurfaced in the mid-1980s and had escalated ever since. In 1987, the NAACP launched a campaign to lower Confederate flags from Southern capitols and eventually helped bring Alabama's down. Black cheerleaders refused to carry the rebel flag at college ball games. Schools started banning "Old South" weekends and the playing of "Dixie." In some cities, blacks called for the removal of confederate monuments and rebel street names. And in 1993, black senator Carol Moseley-Braun successfully challenged renewal of the patent for the United Daughters of the Confederacy insignia, which incorporated the Confederacy's political banner.

But this growing militancy provoked a backlash among Southern whites, many of whom already felt aggrieved over the Martin Luther King Jr. holiday, affirmative action, and other race-tinged issues. Self-styled

"Southern heritage" or "Southern nationalist" groups spread like kudzu[7] across the region, preaching the gospel of states' rights, regional pride and reverence for the Confederacy.

These groups also cleverly tapped into the culture of self-esteem and identity politics common across the land. When Spike Lee's movie on Malcolm X launched a wave of "X" clothing, a counter-symbol quickly sprouted on T-shirts and bumper stickers across the white South. It showed the diagonal cross of the rebel flag beside the words "You Wear Your X, I'll Wear Mine."

* * *

By the time Marcus Flippin became a teacher and sports coach at Todd Central in 1992, students were brandishing their separate Xs like duelling pistols. A white kid would show up in a rebel-flag bandanna, a black kid in an X cap. A fight would break out, and the next day still more students would show up wearing Xs and start the cycle over again.

Flippin, one of only three black teachers at the school, became a sounding board for black students. "They'd see on the news about the flag coming down in Alabama, or 'Dixie' being banned," he said, "and they'd come to me and ask, 'How come whites still get away with that stuff here?' "

* * *

A few weeks later, I finally saw Michael's truck, which Hannah drove in one of the half-dozen memorials held in her husband's honor in the weeks following his death. This particular wake was organized by motorcycle clubs in Kentucky and called, with conscious irony, "Freedom Ride '95."[8]

The bikers growled down Guthrie's main street to a vacant lot beside a grain elevator. Several bikers erected a makeshift stage and auctioned leather jackets and other items, with the proceeds donated to the Westerman family. Parked beside the stage was Westerman's truck, with the rebel flag flying from a pole in back. Well-wishers filed solemnly by, poking their pinkies in the small bullet hole in the door and peering at Michael's cowboy hat, perched on the dashboard with the watermelon bubble-gum still stuck to the brim.

7 **kudzu:** a fast-growing vine that is often treated like a weed in the southern United States

8 **Freedom Ride '95:** an allusion to the Freedom Rides of the 1960s which helped to integrate busses in the Southern States

Hannah, a tall, hefty woman with permed strawberry-blond hair, stood impassively beside the cab. I asked her why she thought Michael had displayed the flag. Was it Southern pride?

"He wasn't into all the Confederate history and that," she said, echoing her father. "He didn't, like, dig into it."

"School spirit?"

She smiled. "Michael was glad just to graduate from the place." She said a few of Michael's friends had started flying the flag from their pickups about the time he bought his truck. He decided to do the same.

"Why?"

Hannah shrugged. "He'd do anything to make his truck look sharp. The truck's red. The flag's red. They match."

* * *

[At the end of the trial for Michael's accused killers] as the judge deliberated, the families stood at opposite ends of the courthouse, holding hands and praying. When the judge returned after a ninety-minute recess, the chamber filled with undercover police. There had been anonymous death threats against the judge, and police also feared a post-verdict brawl between the families.

Fingering a Styrofoam coffee cup, the judge spent several minutes staring at a legal pad. Then he read the charges against Freddie, finding him guilty of felony murder, attempted aggravated kidnapping, and civil-rights intimidation. "The court imposes sentence of imprisonment for life," he said. Damien Darden received the same. The third defendant, a fifteen-year-old who had apparently just been along for the ride, was found not guilty on all counts.

Freddie's head slumped on his chest. Damien stared blankly ahead. Behind them, relatives burst into tears, as did the women in the Westerman family. Except for Hannah. Striding out of the courtroom, she paused before a TV camera and declared, "They got what they deserved—well, they deserved to die." But she seemed satisfied by her day in court. "It's about time," she said, "someone who's white got to stand up and say, 'Our civil rights were violated.' "

* * *

On the Sunday after the trial, I went to a service at Guthrie's black Baptist church attended by members of the defendants' families. Several relatives got up to thank the community for their support. "God will deliver his verdict, but in his own good time," Freddie's aunt said. "We look at the little pictures, He takes the big view." Another woman wailed, "I don't want to go to hell, Lord. It's hell here." Then the pastor set the trial in the broad context of black suffering. "We have been o-pressed and de-pressed for over two hundred years," he said. "Ain't nothing change but the years."

After the service, Freddie's mother invited me to her in-laws' house, a small bungalow across from the church. Showing me a picture of Freddie at age two, hugging a Teddy bear, she pondered how her youngest child could have ended up in prison for murder. Perhaps, she said, it was her fault, for losing her job when Freddie was a young teenager; after that, she'd had to move to a rough area of Chicago she described as New Jack City. It was there that her son first got into trouble.

Or maybe adolescent hormones were to blame. "Boys got this thing, showing your manhood, that you're bad," she said. "It's a man thing." But she was also angry that racism and the rebel flag hadn't really been aired at the trial. "The flag and 'n—r'-calling—you can deny that it hurts you, but it builds up," she said. "You keeping putting it on people, it's going to blow up."

* * *

Ten minutes up the road, at the Westermans' house in flat farmland north of Guthrie, fourteen rebel flags were on display. One flew at half-mast, the others draped across porch furniture. Inside, Hannah sat with her in-laws watching Oprah as her twin children frolicked on the floor. One toddler wore a rebel-flag shirt: "American by Birth, Rebel by the Grace of God." The den was also cluttered with Confederate parapher-nalia, most of it gifts from well-wishers across the South.

Michael's mother, JoAnn, joined us. A wiry woman of forty, she said she now took tranquilizers and had entered counseling with her husband to deal with their son's death. Returning to work at the garment factory had also been tough. "Blacks I consider myself close to, deep down inside there's something in between us now," she said. "We leave that void there and don't discuss it."

Michael's father, David, offered to show me a home video. Images of Michael rolled across the TV screen: as a baby, as a seventh-grader on the football team, at home making a science-fair telegraph with his father, at the senior prom with Hannah, and finally, cradling his newborn twins. David Westerman began to cry. A modest, soft-spoken man, he was, like Freddie's mother, still trying to make sense of what had happened to his son.

"Look at this," he said, opening an album of family history he'd been given by his sister, Brenda Arms. David ran his finger along a list of rebel ancestors: one captured, another shot dead at Gettysburg, and a private "killed in action, 24th May, 1862." His age was listed as nineteen.

"Just like Michael," David said. He wiped his eyes. "They say that war ended a long time ago. But around here it's like it's still going on."

Street fighters in Northern Ireland.

Change of Heart

Patrick Rogers

Northern Ireland has been in a state of civil war since the 1500s, when England seized land from the Irish Catholics and gave it to British Protestants. The most recent conflict started in 1921 when Ireland was divided with six northern counties remaining under English Protestant control. Some Catholics formed a guerrilla group, the Irish Republican Army, to fight for independence from the British.

Violence continues to this day. A truce was negotiated by both sides in the Good Friday Accords of 1998. The plan to develop a government agreeable to both the British Protestants and the Irish Catholics was overwhelmingly approved by voters.

If he had grown up in a city other than Londonderry, Shane Paul O'Doherty might have considered the priesthood. He attended mass several times a week as a boy, recited the rosary every night and donned lacy robes to sing Latin hymns in the choir of St. Eugene's Cathedral, the dark stone edifice that towered above his home on a tidy street in Northern Ireland's second-largest city. "Life was very much bound up with God, religion and that cathedral," says O'Doherty, 43.

But events in Londonderry—which, reflecting the ancient rift dividing its citizens, Catholics call simply Derry—steered O'Doherty in a different direction. Beginning in the late 1960s, Catholics took to the streets to protest centuries of political and economic domination by the city's Protestant minority. Their marches erupted into violent confrontations with Protestant police, beginning the Troubles that plague Northern Ireland to this day.

Young O'Doherty yearned to take part in the struggle. At age 10, he hid a note in the attic of his family's Georgian-style townhouse on Clarendon Street: "When I grow up," he wrote, "I want to fight, and if necessary, die for Ireland's freedom." As it happened, he didn't have to wait long. On his way to school one morning in 1970, O'Doherty, then 15, was asked by his best friend to join the Irish Republican Army with him. For the next five years he used guns, land mines and mail bombs to injure civilians, soldiers and policemen. But O'Doherty, now a computer trainer and freelance journalist in Dublin, made what he considers his most enduring contribution to his people's quest for justice only after he was arrested and sentenced to life in prison. With time to reflect on his crimes, he embarked on a remarkable journey from terrorist to peace-maker. He wrote letters of apology to his victims, denounced terrorism and publicly challenged the IRA, from which he officially resigned in 1978, to lay down its arms.

Republican extremists have never forgiven him. But for many in his battle-weary country, Shane Paul O'Doherty's message of peace has made him a hero. "He was angry—justly angry—at the injustices in Northern Ireland," says peace activist Mairead Corrigan-Maguire, 54, cowinner of the 1976 Nobel Peace Prize. "But he realized that to kill and hurt is never justified. He had the courage to break ranks."

O'Doherty was raised on one of the few streets in Londonderry where middle-class Catholics and Protestants lived side by side. Yet the line between them was clearly drawn. "In games," he recalls, "we divided fifty-fifty down the middle." O'Doherty describes his late father, Bernard, a teacher at a Christian Brothers elementary school, and his mother, Sarah, now 82, who raised the couple's eight children, as peace loving but patriotic. His father spoke admiringly of one of Shane's uncles who had fought in the 1919-21 war that won Ireland—all but the six counties of the North—her independence from Britain. They also bitterly resented the chronic unemployment among the city's working-class Catholics, many of whom crowded into tiny rented houses without indoor plumbing. "There wasn't a Catholic in Derry who didn't think they were being looked down upon," he says.

On the night after the morning he decided to become a terrorist,

Funeral procession in Northern Ireland, 1972.

O'Doherty reported to a house in the Bogside
Catholic ghetto, scene of Londonderry's fiercest rioting, and was sworn
into the Provisional Irish Republican Army. Several weeks later two commanders appeared at his family's house and asked him to hide a backpack containing a bomb. Instead he placed the crude device at
the door of a police dormitory at 3 a.m., causing extensive damage. "I did-
n't want to end up like my father, who only heard about the struggle," he
says. "I wanted to be my uncle, at the heart of it all, getting the kudos."

After a stern lecture from his commanders about discipline,
O'Doherty was welcomed into the inner circle of the IRA's Derry Brigade.
Each morning he went to school; after classes he shot at British soldiers
on patrol and used American munitions manuals to make bombs he
planted on downtown streets. "They were delighted to have someone
who rocked and rolled," he says of his colleagues.

By the time 14 Catholics were shot and killed by British troops during
a demonstration on Jan. 30, 1972—Bloody Sunday, as it came to be
known—O'Doherty had lost all qualms about attacking the soldiers: "I
saw it as time for Irish people to fight for freedom and get the [British]
b—s out of here." When civilians, too, were hurt by his blasts, he recalled
the commander who'd told him, "You can't make an omelette without
breaking eggs."

In 1973, armed with a pocketful of English currency and a copy of
Who's Who, O'Doherty accepted a special assignment. Working from a
small apartment in London, he mailed some 50 letter bombs to British
politicians and military officers. Some reached their targets, but many
injured security guards and secretaries, including a woman at the British
Embassy in Washington whose left hand was blown off when she

opened a parcel that August.

Police used fingerprints to link the bombings to O'Doherty, and in 1976 he was convicted and sentenced to 30 consecutive life terms in prison. Like many IRA prisoners, he refused to wear the uniform given to common criminals. As a result he spent nearly 15 months naked in solitary confinement. That stretch, O'Doherty says, gave him time to study philosophy — and to examine his conscience. "I read the Bible for the first time and felt tremendous guilt," he says. "I read the statement of the victims at my trial and was utterly damned. My conscience was giving me no ease about hurting innocent people, and I even started to question whether there's any such thing as a legitimate target."

While in prison, O'Doherty resigned from the IRA and, in an open letter published in the Derry Journal in 1978, called on the group to lay down its arms. In retaliation, fellow IRA prisoners refused to talk to him for eight years. O'Doherty was released in 1989, after a letter-writing campaign on his behalf by sympathetic politicians and clerics. Still, not everyone accepted his redemption. Said Derek Woodward, a Bank of England guard who had lost an eye and a hand to one of O'Doherty's bombs: "[He] comes out, goes to university and carries on a perfectly lovely life, but I have still got to serve my life sentence."

After his release, O'Doherty studied at Trinity College in Dublin, where he earned a degree in English literature in 1993, wrote a bestselling autobiography and became an outspoken advocate of peace in the North. In class in 1991, he caught the attention of a recently arrived Chicagoan; on their first date she assumed O'Doherty's talk of the IRA had to do with Individual Retirement Accounts. "I thought he was studying to be an accountant!" says medieval-literature instructor Mickey Sweeney O'Doherty, 30, who married him in 1995, convinced of his conversion to nonviolence. "He doesn't like to be wrong, and to discover he was so very wrong must have been painful."

Visiting Londonderry on a bright spring day this year, O'Doherty walked through gritty streets where he had once carried a gun, pausing to ask a group of teenagers what they thought of the historic peace proposal. "I'm for it," shouted one before rushing back to his soccer game. For O'Doherty, who has talked about his life to youth groups all over Ireland, the answer was encouraging. "I frequently think of friends who died in the armed struggle," he says. "What, I ask them, did you die for? They died so that we might learn the truth: that armed struggle is a lie." ⸸

Slavery in Sudan

Hilary MacKenzie

Though slavery has been abolished in most of the world, there are still countries where it is tolerated by the national government. The United Nations condemns slavery as a violation of human rights but often has no way to enforce the international law forbidding it.

Slavery is worse than death," says Ayom Ayom, 18. He should know. His country, the African nation of Sudan, is home to one of the world's last thriving slave markets. Earlier this year, Ayom barely escaped capture when raiders encircled the camp where he and his tribe take livestock to water. The slave traders rounded up 510 children and 20,000 head of cattle.

One of those captured was 20-year-old Wol Buong Arol. For two days, Wol was lassoed and dragged behind horses, en route to being sold. But when the raider got distracted haggling over cattle, Wol dodged behind a mango tree and ran for his life. Angry red rope burns still scar his wrists from where he was tied.

The slave trade in Sudan is fueled by the country's long-running civil war. For all but 10 years since gaining independence in 1956, Africa's largest country has been wracked by internal conflict. Trafficking in humans has thrived during the fighting, especially in the 1990s, says Jemera Rone, a Sudan expert at Human Rights Watch, a human-rights organization.

The war pits the national government in Khartoum, which is dominated by northern Arab Muslims, against southern rebels, mainly black Christians, who are fighting for autonomy. The north wants to impose

Muslim slave
trader

Islam and the Arabic language on the south, while the south, led by the Sudan People's Liberation Army (SPLA), wants a secular democratic government. Over the last 15 years, more than 1.5 million Sudanese have been killed, and some 4 million more have been displaced by the fighting.

The slave trade has been carried out by Arab militias called murahaleen, who conduct military-style raids on civilian villages and cattle camps. They descend on horseback, armed with government-issued automatic weapons, and capture hundred of civilians at a time, for sale into slavery.

Humans-rights groups and United Nations (UN) investigators say the militias are supported by the Sudanese government. The government denies any connection to them and also denies that slavery exists within its borders. Sudanese officials blame intertribal disputes for what they describe as the taking of prisoners.

Most of those taken are Dinka, a million-member tribe that forms the largest ethnic group in southern Sudan. Dinka are targets because they form the backbone of the SPLA and inhabit the Bahr el Ghazal, the region that borders the Arab-dominated north.

The raids are conducted in areas where there are no SPLA troops. "The objective is not to kill enemy troops but to enslave 'enemy' civilians and weaken the Dinka, economically and socially," Rone says.

Those abducted are forced to walk, hands bound together, behind horses to camps in the north.

"Thousands of women and children have their ankle tendons severed to disable them so they cannot escape," says Steven Wondu, an SPLA official.

Although the number of slaves is difficult to ascertain, human-rights groups estimate that from 30,000 to 90,000 Sudanese have been enslaved, mostly women and children. They are given Arabic names, and sold to Arab masters, says the Reverend Cal Bombay, vice president of Crossroads, a Christian nonprofit group based in Toronto, Canada. Young men, meanwhile, are killed or forced into military service, brainwashed into fighting against their own people.

Many of the Dinka resort to selling their cattle to try to buy slaves back into freedom. Apin Apin Akot recalls the day when the murahaleen captured his wife and two children. He was out tending the cattle and returned to find his village razed and his family gone. He sold his cows and walked north for seven days, paying bribes to learn where his family was. When he confronted the slave trader, he was told he had only enough money to buy back his wife and youngest daughter. The other daughter, 9-year-old Akec, watched her father walk away without her.

Months later, Apin returned with money Bombay and others had raised to free Akec. "I knew you'd come back and get me," the girl said, her cheeks scarred from beatings she'd endured while in captivity.

The treatment of slaves is horrifying, Bombay says. Boys who tried to escape have had their hands and feet macheted off. Girls, too, have been brutally mutilated. Most slaves, he says, live like dogs, on the street, begging for scraps of food.

The UN, the United States, and other countries have condemned the slave trading, but they have taken little action. In November 1997, the U.S. imposed economic sanctions on Sudan to protest its abysmal human-rights record, including its support for slavery. But critics say that neither the U.S. nor the UN has actively pressed the issue.

As much as the slavery itself, that silence troubles many activists. "Human beings by their very nature prefer to believe that it doesn't exist," says the SPLA's Wondu. "The bitter truth is that trading in humans is a booming commercial enterprise in Sudan today."

Female slaves wait for their freedom to be purchased.

AT GETTYSBURG

LINDA PASTAN

These fields can never be
simply themselves. Their green
seems such a tender green,
their contours so significant
to the tourists who stare

towards the far range of mountains
as if they are listening
to the page of history tearing
or to what they know themselves of warfare
between brothers. In this scenery

cows and cannons stand side by side
and motionless, as if they had grown here.
The cannons on their simple wheels
resemble farm carts, children
climb them. Thus function disappears almost entirely

into form, and what is left under
the impartial blue of the sky is a landscape
where dandelions lie in the tall grass
like so many spent cartridges, turning
at last to the smoke

of puffballs; where the only red
visible comes at sunset;
where the earth has grown so lovely
it seems to forgive us even as we are learning
to forgive ourselves.

YOUNG SOLDIER
painted 1864
Winslow Homer

Winslow Homer (1836-1910) *Young Soldier: Separate Study of a Soldier Giving Water to a Wounded Companion.* 1861. Oil, gouache, black crayon on canvas, 14 7/8 x 6 7/8 inches. Cooper-Hewitt, National Design Museum, Smithsonian Institution/Art Resource, NY. Photo by Ken Pelka, gift of Charles Savage Homer, 1912-12-110.

RESPONDING TO CLUSTER FOUR

Thinking Skill SYNTHESIZING

1. Each of the other clusters in this book is introduced by a question that is meant to help readers focus their thinking about the selections. What do you think the question for cluster four should be?

2. How do you think the selections in this cluster should be taught? Demonstrate your ideas by joining with your classmates to:

   a) create discussion questions

   b) lead discussions about the selections

   c) develop vocabulary quizzes

   d) prepare a cluster quiz

REFLECTING ON *A HOUSE DIVIDED:*

Essential Question WHY IS THE CIVIL WAR CONSIDERED A DEFINING MOMENT IN AMERICAN HISTORY?

Reflecting on this book as a whole provides an opportunity for independent learning and the application of the critical thinking skill, synthesis. *Synthesizing* means examining all the things you have learned from this book and combining them to form a richer and more meaningful view of America's Civil War. There are many ways to demonstrate what you know about the Civil War. Here are some possibilities. Your teacher may provide others.

1. Using the information in this book, and in other books, movies and television shows you might have seen, write a persuasive essay answering the essential question: Why is the Civil War considered a defining moment in American history? Use examples to support your arguments.

2. Individually or in small groups, develop an independent project that demonstrates your knowledge of the Civil War. For example, you might stage a debate Resolved: "The Civil War ended in 1865." Other options might include a music video, dance, poem, performance, drama, or artistic rendering.

AUTHOR BIOGRAPHIES

LOUISA MAY ALCOTT Born in 1832 of educated and idealistic but impoverished parents, Louisa May Alcott began working at an early age to help support the family. She worked as a teacher, governess, domestic servant, traveling companion, and seamstress, and also wrote stories for a local journal. In 1866, a publishing firm asked her to write a story for girls, and Alcott did so by fictionalizing her own childhood. The resulting novel, entitled *Little Women*, became an immediate success. Alcott went on to write several more novels for children, several novels for adult women, and biographical accounts of her experiences. She also was active in the women's suffrage movement. She died in 1888, two days after the death of her beloved father.

RAY BRADBURY Describing the act of writing as "a fever—something I must do," Ray Bradbury acknowledges that he always has "some new fever developing, some new love to follow and bring to life." As if to back up that claim, he wrote his first story at age 11, on butcher paper. Since then, Bradbury has published more than 500 short stories, novels, plays, screenplays, television scripts, and poems. Many, such as *The Martian Chronicles, The Illustrated Man, Fahrenheit 451*, and *Something Wicked This Way Comes*, have been best sellers. All have been wildly creative, blending contemporary issues with fantastical science fiction to make observations about the way we live today. Among his many awards are the O. Henry Memorial Award, the Benjamin Franklin Award, the World Fantasy Award for lifetime achievement, and the Grand Master Award from the Science Fiction Writers of America. He received the National Book Foundation Medal for his distinguished contribution to American letters.

BRUCE CATTON A historian best known for his American Civil War trilogy, *The Coming Fury, The Terrible Swift Sword*, and *Never Call Retreat*, Bruce Catton was born in 1899 in Michigan. He spent most of his life in the Midwest. As a young man, he served in the navy during World War I, then began earning a living as a freelance writer. Catton won a Pulitzer Prize and the National Book Award for *A Stillness at Appomattox* and a special Pulitzer citation in 1961 for *The American Heritage Picture History of the Civil War*. He died in Michigan in 1978.

ROBERT W. CHAMBERS Born in Brooklyn in 1865, Robert W. Chambers was a direct descendant of Roger Williams, the founder of Rhode Island. As part of a wealthy and aristocratic family, he was expected to excel. Chambers attended art school and then studied art in Paris. He returned to the United States and sold his illustrations to leading American magazines then abruptly turned to writing. Chambers published a number of horror stories, which became extremely popular. Then he expanded his range, writing historical fiction, short stories, poems, and essays, as well as novels of all sorts. Over the course of his lifetime, he became one of the most successful fiction writers of the 1920s and 1930s. Chambers died in 1933.

MARY BOYKIN CHESTNUT During her lifetime, Mary Chestnut was a proper southern lady. She had been educated in the liberal arts and in "feminine accomplishments" such as needlepoint, drawing, and music. The wife of a senator, she was witty, well traveled, and at home among the world's elite. Yet Chestnut's diaries reveal a more complex figure, one who taught slaves to read and write and came to dislike slavery intensely. When the Civil War threw her family into poverty, Chestnut hoped to earn a living by writing her memoirs, but she died before she was able to finish them. Her friends rescued them from obscurity and gave to the world Chestnut's picture of life in the Civil War South.

PAUL LAWRENCE DUNBAR The first African American writer to achieve both literary and financial success as a writer, Paul Lawrence Dunbar was born in 1872, the son of a former slave. He earned a high school diploma, then took a job as an elevator operator to support himself. In 1893 he published his first book of poems, and in 1895 he published his second, both at his own expense. The second book won the attention of critic William Dean Howells, who praised his use of African American dialect and encouraged Dunbar to continue writing. Dunbar's third book of poems, *Lyrics of Lowly Life*, opened with a preface by Howells. Dunbar struggled against tuberculosis throughout most of his adult life and finally died of the disease at age 33. After his death, he was both praised as a poet of "Negro folk life" and disparaged as a sell-out to white audiences. Today, he is remembered as one of the leading lights of the Harlem Renaissance.

F. SCOTT FITZGERALD Born in 1898 of affluent parents, F. Scott Fitzgerald grew up on the edge of polite society. He attended Princeton but spent more time and energy writing than attending classes, and he never earned a degree. He joined the army in 1917 and wrote a novel while awaiting deployment to Europe. The novel was politely rejected. He fell in love with southern belle Zelda Sayre but failed to win her hand until a later novel, *This Side of Paradise*, won him both critical success and praise. Scott and Zelda, as the couple were known, embarked on a glamorous but dissolute life among jazz-age luminaries here and abroad. Though Fitzgerald sold numerous short stories, novels, and screenplays, financial security eluded him. He was often drunk and almost always in debt, and his wife, Zelda, spent much of her adult life in sanitariums. Fitzgerald died in 1940, but his work did not begin to enjoy serious critical appreciation until after World War II.

SUSAN HAYES A senior editor with the National Geographic Society, Susan Hayes has written articles for their Web site, National Geographic Kids, as well as reports for *Scholastic* magazine.

TONY HORWITZ When writing about the South and the Civil War as a third grader, Tony Horwitz began his account this way: "The War was started when after all the states had sececed (sic)." Though his spelling—and his understanding of history—improved greatly over time, Horwitz never lost his early enthusiasm for writing stories about war. As a foreign correspondent for the *Wall Street Journal*, Horwitz spent ten years writing about conflicts in Bosnia, the Middle East, Africa, and Northern Ireland. He also reports on national issues. He has won the Pulitzer Prize and the Overseas Press Club Award for his work. Currently, Horwitz works as a staff writer for the *New Yorker*.

ANDREW HUDGINS Although born in Texas, Andrew Hudgins spent most of his childhood in Alabama. After college he moved to Iowa and earned an M.F.A. from the University of Iowa. His first collection of poems was nominated for the Pulitzer Prize. Later works have won the Poet's Prize and the National Book Award. Hudgins has also written a collection of personal essays. In addition to writing, he teaches literature and writing at the University of Cincinnati.

ROBERT E. LEE The son of a revolutionary war hero, Robert E. Lee began his career as an army engineer, later joining the cavalry to improve his prospects. When Virginia seceded from the Union, Lee resigned his commission. He became the commander of Virginia's military forces, advisor to confederate President Jefferson Davis, and then commander in chief of the Confederacy. Though he fought a losing war, Lee was admired for his courage and skill and for holding off Union forces in Virginia for almost three years. After the war, Lee took a position as president of Washington College (now Washington and Lee University) in Lexington, Virginia. He died in 1870 of heart disease. More than 100 years later, his United States citizenship was officially restored.

ABRAHAM LINCOLN The sixteenth President of the United States, Abraham Lincoln was born in a log cabin and reared in rural Kentucky, Indiana, and Illinois. He educated himself while working on a farm and as a store clerk in New Salem, Illinois. Eventually, he became a lawyer, then a legislator. In 1858, Lincoln debated Stephen A. Douglas in a race for a Senate seat. Lincoln lost the election, but made a name for himself and later secured the 1860 Republican nomination for President. After winning the presidential election, Lincoln presided over the Civil War. He is best known for issuing the Emancipation Proclamation that freed America's slaves. Lincoln was assassinated in 1865, only days after the official end of the Civil War.

HILARY MACKENZIE is the North American correspondent for Canada's *Saturday Night* Magazine. She writes about global and environmental issues of interest to North Americans.

James McPherson Born in Ohio in 1828, as a young man James McPherson joined the U.S. Army and taught engineering at West Point Military Academy. When the Civil War began, he joined the Union Army and became chief engineer under Ulysses S. Grant. In 1862, he commanded the 2nd division of the Union Army of Tennessee. McPherson was killed in 1864 during the Battle of Atlanta. An able and respected leader, he was mourned by his troops and even by some of his battlefield enemies.

Herman Melville was an American novelist, essayist, and poet who lived from 1819 to 1891. During his own lifetime he was best known for his South Seas adventures. His epic poems and his masterpiece, *Moby Dick*, did not gain the attention of his other works until years after he died. By the time of his death Melville had nearly been forgotten except as a minor writer of popular literature. Critics began to reevaluate *Moby Dick* in the 1920s, and today Melville is considered one of the most important figures in American literature.

Linda Pastan Born in New York in 1954, poet Linda Pastan says that "by age 10 or 11, I knew I wanted to spend my life writing. But I don't think I knew that real people could be 'writers' until much later." Pastan has published numerous volumes of poetry, won countless prizes, and was named poet laureate of Maryland from 1991 to 1994. Exploring the themes of family, children, the passage of time, and the beauty of nature, Pastan manages to make everyday life worth writing—and reading—about. *The San Francisco Review of Books* describes her as "returning to the role of the poet as it served the human race for centuries: to fuel our thinking, show us our world in new ways, and to get us to feel more intensely about the ordinary."

Gary Paulsen At the age of 14, Gary Paulsen ran away from an unhappy home and joined the circus. His taste for adventure led him to work as a farmhand, engineer, construction worker, truck driver, rancher, sailor, and dog trainer for the Iditarod, an Alaskan dogsled race. Some of these life experiences are reflected in the more than 175 books he has written for children and young adults. His novels *Hatchet, Dogsong,* and *The Winter Room* are all Newbery Honor books. What keeps the author at his desk for up to 20 hours a day? As one biographer put it, "It is Paulsen's overwhelming belief in young people that drives him to write."

Horace Porter Born in 1837 and educated at West Point, Horace Porter was both a soldier and a diplomat. Porter served in the Union Army during the Civil War. He earned the Congressional Medal of Honor for his actions at the Battle of Chickamauga. Porter wrote two books about his early military experiences. After the war, he served as personal secretary to President Ulysses S. Grant and then as the U.S. ambassador to France. He died in 1921.

WILLIAM CLARKE QUANTRILL Born in 1837, William Clarke Quantrill began his professional life as a schoolteacher, but later became infamous as a gambler, murderer, and horse thief. When the Civil War erupted, Quantrill gathered a group of raiders and fought guerrilla-style for the Confederacy. Quantrill and his raiders killed 183 men and boys in the bloody Lawrence, Kansas, massacre. When Union forces began to rout the Confederates, Quantrill fled to Texas, and his raiders broke up into smaller bands of outlaws. Quantrill died during a raid in Kentucky in 1865 and became a popular folk hero. His popularity rubbed off on ex-raiders Frank and Jesse James and on the Younger brothers, outlaws who used Quantrill's hit-and-run methods to rob banks and trains.

WILLIAM HOWARD RUSSELL Born in 1821 in Dublin County and educated at Trinity College in Ireland and at Cambridge in England, William Howard Russell was an Irish journalist. In 1854, he became the first foreign correspondent for the London *Times*. Russell witnessed, among other things, the outbreak of the Crimean War, the coronation of Tsar Alexander II in Russia, the American Civil War, and the Franco-Prussian War. His telegraph dispatches brought war news to his readers with an immediacy never before experienced. Russell was knighted in May 1895 and died in 1907.

GIDEON WELLES Born the son of a New England merchant in 1802, Gideon Welles intended to study law but instead became part-owner and editor of the Hartford *Times*. After making that paper one of New England's leading Democratic papers, he joined the Connecticut state legislature as a Democrat. In 1854, Welles joined the newly formed Republican party and founded a newspaper espousing its ideals. Lincoln, the first Republican President, made Welles the Secretary of the Navy. Under Welles, this navy was able to blockade the southern coast of the United States. Welles left this position in 1869 and wrote several nonfiction books before his death in 1878. He also wrote faithfully in his diary, which was published in 1911.

ADDITIONAL READING

Abraham's Battle: A Novel of Gettysburg, Sara Harrell Banks. The Civil War is experienced through the eyes of Abraham Small, a former slave, and Lamar Cooper, a young Confederate soldier. ©1999

Across Five Aprils, Irene Hunt. The heartache and agony of the Civil War as reflected in the life of a young Illinois boy. ©1986

The American Civil War: A House Divided, Edward F. Dolan. This books focuses on the battles, strategies, and technological advances that developed during the Civil War, providing a concise overview of the conflicts that divided our nation. ©1997

Before the Creeks Ran Red, Carolyn Reeder. Through the eyes of three different boys, three linked novellas explore the tumultuous times beginning with the secession of South Carolina and leading up to the first major battle of the Civil War. ©2003

Behind the Blue and Gray: The Soldier's Life in the Civil War, Delia Ray. Drawing on letters, diaries, eyewitness accounts, and vintage photographs, *Behind the Blue and Gray* explores the extraordinary experiences of common soldiers from all walks of life. ©1996

Bound for the Promised Land: Harriet Tubman, Portrait of an American Heroine, Katherine Larson. Harriet Tubman is one of the giants of American history—a fearless visionary who led scores of her fellow slaves to freedom and battled courageously behind enemy lines during the Civil War. ©2003

The Boys' War, Jim Murphy. First-hand accounts, including diary entries and personal letters, describe the experiences of boys 16 years old or younger who fought in the Civil War. More than 50 archival photographs. ©1990

Braving the Fire, John B. Severance. Jem joins the Union Army but is not sure of his motives or what he hopes to accomplish, particularly since the Civil War has divided his family and caused much violence and confusion in his life. ©2002

Bright Freedom's Song: A Story of the Underground Railroad, Gloria Houston. In the years before the Civil War, Bright discovers that her parents are providing a safe house for the Underground Railroad, and she helps to save a runaway slave named Marcus. ©1998

"Bury Me Not in a Land of Slaves": African-Americans in the Time of Reconstruction, Joyce Hansen. This book is an account of African American life in the period of Reconstruction following the Civil War, based on first-person narratives, contemporary documents, and other historical sources. ©2000

Civil War Journal: The Leaders, William C. Davis & Brian C. Pohanka, eds. Presented by the History Channel. ©2003

Cold Mountain, Charles Frazier. Adult Civil War novel about a man who leaves an army hospital and walks out of the war back to his beloved Cold Mountain and the woman he loves. Some mature content. ©1998

Days of Jubilee: The End of Slavery in the United States, Patricia C. & Frederick L. McKissack. This book uses slave narratives, letters, diaries, military orders, and other documents to chronicle the various stages leading to the emancipation of slaves in the United States. ©2003

Evvy's Civil War, Miriam Brenaman. In Virginia in 1860, on the verge of the Civil War, 14-year-old Evvy chafes at the restrictions that her society places on both women and slaves. ©2002

From Slave Ship to Freedom Road, Julius Lester. Here is a depiction of the course of slavery, beginning with the ships sailing from Africa on the notorious Middle Passage and continuing through the Civil War. ©2000

Gods and Generals, Jeff M. Shaara. This is the prequel to the Civil War epic, *Killer Angels*, written by the author's father. It follows the lives of Robert E. Lee, Stonewall Jackson, Winfield Scott Hancock, and Joshua Chamberlain from 1858 to 1863. ©1996

Gone with the Wind, Margaret Mitchell. Flaming epic of Civil War times. ©1993

Harriet Tubman: Conductor on the Underground Railroad, Ann Petry. The story of the courageous black woman who first escaped to freedom alone on the Underground Railroad and then went back again and again to lead others to freedom. ©1971

Hear the Wind Blow: A Novel of the Civil War, Mary Downing Hahn. With their mother dead and their home burned, a 13-year-old boy and his little sister set out across Virginia in search of relatives during the final days of the Civil War. ©2003

The House of Dies Drear, Virginia Hamilton. An African American family tries to unravel the secrets of its new home, which was once a stop on the Underground Railroad. ©1984

In My Father's House, Ann Rinaldi. An insightful historical novel set during the Civil War that looks at a girl's struggle to keep her family together and to accept her stepfather's beliefs about slavery and the war. ©1993

Jayhawker, Patricia Beatty. In the early years of the Civil War, teenage Kansas farm boy Lije Tulley becomes a Jayhawker, an abolitionist raider, freeing slaves from the neighboring state of Missouri. He then goes undercover there as a spy. ©1995

Jubilee, Margaret Walker. A Civil War novel that chronicles the triumph of a free spirit over many kinds of bondage. ©1967

Last Full Measure, Jeff M. Shaara. Extensive historical Civil War fiction. Sequel to his father's book *Killer Angels*. ©2000

The Last Silk Dress, Ann Rinaldi. In this historical account, 14-year-old Susan Chilmark shows support for the Confederacy during the Civil War by collecting silk dresses to create a huge hot-air balloon in which to spy on the enemy. ©1990

Mountain Valor, Gloria Houston. With her father and brothers gone to serve in the Civil War and her mother sick, Valor ignores what is proper behavior for a teenage girl and fights to defend her North Carolina mountain farm. ©1996

Mr. Lincoln's Drummer, G. Clifton Wisler. Accurate details give a true picture of the Civil War and the courage of 10-year-old Willie Johnston, who served as a drummer boy and who was awarded the Congressional Medal of Honor and was asked to play his drum for President Lincoln. ©1997

A Nation Torn: The Story of How the Civil War Began, Delia Ray. Vividly describes the crucial events leading up to the Civil War and brings to life the unforgettable individuals of that era—from peacemaker Henry Clay to writer Harriet Beecher Stowe to abolitionist John Brown. ©1996

The Red Badge of Courage, Stephen Crane. A young Civil War recruit is bewildered by the mad pattern of battle. ©1979

Red Cap, G. Clifton Wisler. Set in 1864, this work is based on the life of 15-year-old Union drummer boy Ransom J. Powell who was imprisoned at Andersonville, the notorious Confederate prison located at Camp Sumter. ©1994

The River Between Us, Richard Peck. Set during the first year of the Civil War and told from a civilian perspective, this is the story of the lifelong impact that one person can have on another. ©2003

Robert E. Lee: Southern Hero of the Civil War, Mona Kerby. Historical American biographies. ©1997

Send One Angel Down, Virginia F. Schwartz. In the pre-Civil War South, a young slave tries to shield the horrors of slavery from his younger cousin, a light-skinned slave who is the daughter of the plantation owner. ©2000

A Separate Battle: Women and the Civil War, Ina Chang. From slave women to abolitionists, spies, and soldiers, courageous women such as Sojourner Truth, Harriet Tubman, and Clara Barton played fascinating and vital roles in the Civil War, and in doing so, transformed their own lives. ©1996

Soldier's Heart, Gary Paulsen. Eager to enlist, 15-year-old Charley has a change of heart after experiencing both the physical and mental anguish of Civil War combat. ©1998

Sound the Jubilee, Sandra Forrester. A slave and her family find refuge on Roanoke Island, North Carolina, during the Civil War. ©1997

Vicksburg: The Battle That Won the Civil War, Mary Ann Fraser. This book describes the events before, during, and after the key Civil War battle of Vicksburg. ©1999

With Every Drop of Blood, James Lincoln Collier & Christopher Collier. A black Yankee soldier captures a white Confederate. IRA Teacher's Choice. ©1997

ACKNOWLEDGMENTS

Text Credits CONTINUED FROM PAGE 2   Excerpts from *Confederates in the Attic* by Tony Horwitz. Copyright © 1998 by Tony Horwitz. Reprinted by permission of Pantheon Books, a division of Random House, Inc.

"The Great Draft Riots" by Susan Hayes. From *Scholastic Update*, September 7, 1998 issue. Copyright © 1998 by Scholastic, Inc. Reprinted by permission of Scholastic, Inc.

From *Marching Toward Freedom: The Negro in the Civil War* by James M. McPherson. Copyright © 1967, 1965 by James M. McPherson. Reprinted by permission of Alfred A. Knopf, Inc.

Diary entries from *Mary Chesnut's Civil War*, edited by C. Vann Woodward (Yale University Press, 1981). Reprinted by permission of Yale University Press.

From *Reflections on the Civil War* by Bruce Catton. Copyright © 1981 by Gerald Dickler as the executor of the estate of Bruce Catton and John Leckley. Used by permission of Doubleday, a division of Random House, Inc.

"Slavery in Sudan" by Hilary MacKenzie. From *Scholastic Update*, December 14, 1998 issue. Copyright © 1998 by Scholastic, Inc. Reprinted by permission of Scholastic, Inc.

"Gettysburg" from *Soldier's Heart* by Gary Paulsen. Copyright © 1998 by Gary Paulsen. Used by permission of Random House Children's Books, a division of Random House, Inc.

Every reasonable effort has been made to properly acknowledge ownership of all material used. Any omissions or mistakes are not intentional and, if brought to the publisher's attention, will be corrected in future editions.

Photo and Art Credits   Cover and Title Page: Larry Rivers, *Last Civil War Veteran*, 1961. Oil on canvas. ©Larry Rivers/Licensed by VAGA, New York, NY/Marlborough Gallery, NY. Pages 3, 4-5: George N. Barnard, courtesy Medford Historical Society, Medford, MA. Page 4: L, Herbert Barrow Wheary Collection; R, courtesy George Eastman House. Page 9: T, Wm. B. T. Trego, *The Rescue of the Colors*, © copyright The Bucks County Historical Society, 1999; B, Stock Montage, Inc. Page 10: T, courtesy George Eastman House; B, Library of Congress. Page 11: T, ©copyright President & Fellows of Harvard College, Peabody Museum, Harvard University 1978; B, The Granger Collection. Page 12: John Ferguson Weir (1841-1926) *Forging the Shaft: a Welding Heat*. Oil on canvas, 52 x 73 1/4 inches. The Metropolitan Museum of Art, gift of Lyman G. Bloomingdale, 1901. Page 13: The Granger Collection. Pages 14 T, 17 ML: The Arthur and Elizabeth Schlesinger Library on the History of Women in America, Radcliffe Institute for Advanced Study, Harvard University, Cambridge; B, Corbis/Bettmann. Pages 15, 17 MR (Detail): George Caleb Bingham, *Order No. 11*, ca. 1865-70. Oil on canvas, 55 1/2 x 78 1/2 inches. The Edwin and Virginia Irwin Memorial, Cincinnati Art Museum. Pages 16 MR, 63: Massachusetts Commandery, Military Order of the Loyal Legion and the U.S. Army Military History Institute. Page 16 BR and BL: The Granger Collection. Page 17: L, Corbis/Bettmann; R, Boston Athenaeum; BL, Baldwin H. Ward, Corbis/Bettmann; BM, The Granger Collection; BR, The Lincoln Museum, Fort Wayne, IN. Page 18: TR, TL, Corbis/Bettmann; BL, Stock Montage, Inc. Page 19: TR, The Granger Collection; BL, Corbis; BR, pages 110-111: Alonzo Chappel (1820-1887) *The Last Hours of Lincoln* (1868) 1971.177, courtesy Chicago Historical Society. Page 21: The Granger Collection. Page 22: Courtesy Beverly R. Robinson Collection, United States Naval Academy Museum. Pages 22-23: Courtesy South Caroliniana Library, University of South Carolina, Columbia. Page 24: Courtesy Mulberry Plantation, Camden, SC. Page 28: Collection of James Frasca. Page 31: Museum of the Confederacy, Richmond. Photo by Larry Sherer from *The American Story: War Between Brothers*, ©1996 Time-Life Books Inc. Page 36: Unidentified photographer, Brady copyright. Courtesy Medford Historical Society, Medford, MA. Page 43: Library of Congress. Pages 44-45: David Gilmour Blythe, *General Abner Doubleday Watching His Troops Cross the Potomac*, (c 1864) Oil on canvas, 30 1/2 x 40 1/4 inches. National Baseball Hall of Fame Library, Cooperstown, NY. Page 48: Library of Congress. Page 48 (background) and 50: Thure de Thulstrap, *The Hornet's Nest*. Seventh Regiment Fund, Inc. Page 55: Courtesy of the Fort St. Joseph Museum. Pages 56-57, 58-59 (Detail): Andre Castaigne, *22nd Negro Regiment, Petersburg, VA*. (Accession # 15134), West Point Museum Collections, United States Military Academy. Page 61: Corbis/Bettmann. Page 62: The Granger Collection. Page 66: Thomas C. Roche, courtesy Medford Historical Society, Medford, MA. Page 68: The Illustrated London News Picture Library. Page 70: The Granger Collection. Pages 72-73: James Walker, *Repulse of Longstreet's Assault at the Battle of Gettysburg*. Collection of Jay P. Altmayer. Page 76: Stock Montage, Inc. Pages 76-77: Timothy O'Sullivan, courtesy George Eastman House. Page 79: T, R, The Granger Collection. Page 81: Unidentified photographer, courtesy Medford Historical Society, Medford, MA. Page 82: Massachusetts Commandery, Military Order of the Loyal Legion and the U.S. Army Military History Institute. Page 86: Collection of Don Troiani. Photo by Larry Sherer from *Voices of the Civil War: Gettysburg*, ©1995 Time-Life Books Inc.